Gretchen Bitterlin
Dennis Johnson
Donna Price
Sylvia Ramirez
K. Lynn Savage, Series Editor

Add Ventures 3

MULTILEVEL WORKSHEETS

with **Ingrid Wisniewska**

CAMBRIDGE
UNIVERSITY PRESS

CAMBRIDGE UNIVERSITY PRESS
Cambridge, New York, Melbourne, Madrid, Cape Town, Singapore, São Paulo, Delhi, Dubai Tokyo

Cambridge University Press
32 Avenue of the Americas, New York, NY 10013–2473, USA

www.cambridge.org
Information on this title: www.cambridge.org/9780521675857

First published 2008
2nd printing 2010

Printed in the United States of America

A catalog record for this publication is available from the British Library.

ISBN 978-0-521-60099-6 pack consisting of Student's Book and Audio CD
ISBN 978-0-521-67960-2 Workbook
ISBN 978-0-521-69891-7 pack consisting of Teacher's Edition and Teacher's Toolkit Audio CD / CD-ROM
ISBN 978-0-521-67730-1 CDs (Audio)
ISBN 978-0-521-67731-8 Cassettes
ISBN 978-0-521-67585-7 Add Ventures

Art direction, book design, photo research, and layout services: Adventure House, NYC
Layout services: TSI Graphics, Effingham, IL

Contents

Introduction

What is *Add Ventures*?

Add Ventures 3 is a book of reproducible worksheets to accompany the *Ventures* Student's Book 3. The worksheets give students additional practice for each lesson in the Student's Book at three levels of difficulty, making it the ideal supplemental material for multilevel classrooms.

For each two-page lesson in the Student's Book, there are three *Add Ventures* worksheets. Each worksheet is designed to provide up to 30 minutes of student work.

What are the three levels of difficulty in *Add Ventures*?

The three tiers in *Add Ventures* allow students who are in the same class but at different levels of English ability to gain confidence and proficiency through level-appropriate tasks.

☑■■ Tier 1 tasks are controlled exercises targeted at students who need the most support as they progress through the Student's Book. A major goal of Tier 1 tasks is to build students' confidence as they work.

■☑■ Tier 2 tasks target students for whom the level of the Student's Book is just right. The exercises are similar to those in the main text. The goal of Tier 2 is to provide additional on-level practice.

■■☑ Tier 3 tasks provide the least support and the greatest challenge. They require more production with fewer cues, and they may extend the content of the lesson in the Student's Book. These tasks target students who move quickly and can easily make connections with previously learned content. The goal of Tier 3 is to challenge students beyond the tasks in the Student's Book.

How do I use *Add Ventures*?

The three tiers of tasks can be structured for *like-ability* (homogeneous) or *cross-ability* (heterogeneous) groups.

In like-ability groupings, students at the *same ability level* work on the same tasks. That is, those students needing the most support work together on Tier 1; students needing the least support work together on Tier 3; students needing more on-level practice work together on Tier 2.

The same or similar content in the tasks across the three tiers of each lesson makes correction easy. Teachers can bring the students together as a whole class to review the answers because the answers on the three worksheets are the same across the tiers.

In cross-ability groupings, students at *different ability levels* work together but use their own level worksheet. Strong students and less strong students work together, enabling peer teaching and peer correction. With cross-ability groupings, the class is usually divided into two groups rather than three. That is, Tier 3 students may work with Tier 1 students while Tier 2 students work in their like-ability group; or Tier 2 students may work with Tier 1 students while Tier 3 students work in their like-ability group. With this cross-ability grouping, feedback on tasks is most often done within the group (student-to-student) rather than as a whole-class activity.

How is *Add Ventures* different from the Workbook for *Ventures*?

The **Workbook** is designed for independent student use outside of class, although it can also be used as additional in-class practice. It provides reinforcement activities at the same level as the lessons in the Student's Book.

Add Ventures is intended for in-class use, particularly in multilevel settings, to target the exercises specific to a student's language-ability level.

Add Ventures worksheets can be used after each lesson in the Student's Book or in conjunction with the Workbook.

Use the Workbook exercises first to determine the appropriate tier of *Add Ventures* to assign to each student. Or use *Add Ventures* first to address individual needs of students prior to assigning the Workbook. In this case, determine the worksheet tier for each student based on the student's understanding of the material in the Student's Book. After successful completion of their *Add Ventures* worksheets, students can do the exercises in the Workbook, either as additional classroom practice or as homework.

A Look at the pictures. Complete the paragraphs. What did Paolo and Andrea do last weekend?

stay home /
watch TV /
eat popcorn

read a book /
go to bed / be
alone all day

Paolo ___*stayed*___ home and _____ TV.
There was a movie on Saturday afternoon. He
_____ popcorn. Then he _____ a book
and _____ to bed early. He _____
alone all day.

meet some
friends / drink
coffee / talk

go to a dance
club / dance
until 1:00 a.m.

Andrea _____ some friends in a café. They
_____ coffee and _____ . Then she
_____ to a dance club with her friends. They
_____ until 1:00 a.m.

B Circle the correct answers.

1. Paolo **is** / **isn't** shy.

2. Paolo **is** / **isn't** outgoing.

3. Paolo **likes** / **dislikes** reading.

4. Andrea **is** / **isn't** friendly.

5. Andrea **is** / **isn't** quiet.

6. Andrea **likes** / **dislikes** being alone.

C Circle the answers about you.

1. I **am** / **am not** outgoing.

2. I **am** / **am not** shy.

3. I **like** / **dislike** staying home.

4. I **like** / **dislike** going out.

Name: _____

Lesson A *Get ready*

A Look at the pictures. Complete the paragraphs. What did Paolo and Andrea do last weekend?

stay home / watch TV / eat popcorn

read a book / go to bed / be alone all day

Paolo *stayed home* and _____ ____ .

There was a movie on Saturday afternoon. He

_____ _____ . Then he _____

____ _____ and _____ ____

_____ early. He ____ _____ all day.

meet some friends / drink coffee / talk

go to a dance club / dance until 1:00 a.m.

Andrea _____ _____ _____

_____ in a café. They _____

_____ and _____ . Then she

_____ to a _____ _____

with her friends. They _____ _____

_____ .

B Circle the correct answers.

1. Paolo is **shy** / **outgoing** / **a party animal**.

2. Paolo isn't **quiet** / **shy** / **outgoing**.

3. Paolo likes **reading** / **dancing** / **going out**.

4. Andrea is **friendly** / **quiet** / **shy**.

5. Andrea isn't **quiet** / **outgoing** / **friendly**.

6. Andrea dislikes **going out** / **dancing** / **being alone**.

C Circle the answers about you.

1. I am **outgoing** / **friendly** / **shy** / **quiet**.

2. I am not **outgoing** / **friendly** / **shy** / **quiet**.

3. I like **staying home** / **going out** / **reading** / **dancing**.

4. I dislike **staying home** / **going out** / **reading** / **dancing**.

Lesson A *Get ready*

A Look at the pictures. Complete the paragraphs. What did Paolo and Andrea do last weekend?

stay home /
watch TV /
eat popcorn

read a book /
go to bed / be
alone all day

Paolo _stayed home and_ _____ .

There was a movie on Saturday afternoon.

He _____ . Then he _____

_____ and _____

_____ early. He _____

_____ .

meet some
friends / drink
coffee / talk

go to a dance
club / dance
until 1:00 a.m.

Andrea _met some friends_ _____ in a café.

They _____ and _____ .

Then she _____

with her friends. They _____

_____ .

B Complete the sentences. Use each word once.

being alone	friendly	outgoing	quiet	reading	shy

1. Paolo is _shy_____ .   4. Andrea is _____ .

2. Paolo isn't _____ .   5. Andrea isn't _____ .

3. Paolo likes _____ .   6. Andrea dislikes _____ .

C Complete the sentences about you.

1. I am _____ .

2. I am not _____ .

3. I like _____ .

4. I dislike _____ .

Name: _____

Lesson B *Verbs + gerunds*

A Write the gerund form of the verbs in the chart.

Drop 'e'	Double consonant	No change
dance → *dancing*	get →	do →
take →	shop →	eat →
write →	swim →	stay →

B Complete the sentences.

1. Nina likes ___*listening*___ to music.
        (listen)

2. Erin enjoys _____ homework.
        (do)

3. Ahmad likes _____ movies.
        (watch)

4. Yolanda and Sam hate _____ bills.
        (pay)

5. Trudy dislikes _____ the garbage.
        (take out)

6. Alma and Lara don't mind _____ the house.
        (clean)

C Write questions and short answers.

1. Nina / like / swimming
   _Does Nina like swimming_____? Yes, _she does____.

2. Ahmad / love / dancing
   _____? Yes, _____.

3. Yolanda and Sam / hate / shopping
   _____? Yes, _____.

4. Trudy / mind / cleaning
   _____? No, _____.

5. Alma and Lara / dislike / playing cards
   _____? No, _____.

D Write two questions to ask a classmate.

Example: _Do you like watching movies_ ?

1. enjoy / play sports _____?

2. like / listen to music _____?

4 **Add Ventures 3**

Lesson B Verbs + gerunds

A Write the gerund forms of the verbs under the correct heading.

dance	do	eat	get	shop	stay	swim	take	write

Drop 'e'	Double consonant	No change
dancing		

B Write sentences.

1. Nina / like / listen to music *Nina likes listening to music.* _____

2. Erin / enjoy / do homework _____

3. Ahmad / like / watch movies _____

4. Yolanda and Sam / hate / pay bills _____

5. Trudy / dislike / take out the garbage _____

6. Alma and Lara / don't mind / clean the house _____

C Write questions using the verb in parentheses. Write short answers.

1. Nina likes swimming.

    (like) *Does Nina like swimming* ? *Yes, she does.*

2. Ahmad loves dancing.

    (love) _____ ? _____

3. Yolanda and Sam hate shopping.

    (hate) _____ ? _____

4. Trudy doesn't mind cleaning.

    (mind) _____ ? _____

5. Alma and Lara enjoy playing cards.

    (dislike) _____ ? _____

D Write two questions to ask a classmate. Use *like*, *dislike*, or *enjoy*.

1. _____ ?

2. _____ ?

Lesson B Verbs + gerunds

A Write the gerund forms in the chart. What is the rule for forming the gerund in each group?

| dance | do | eat | get | shop | swim | stay | take | write |

Rule: _____	Rule: _____	Rule: _____
dancing	*swimming*	*staying*

B Complete the sentences with the verbs in the box. Use the gerund form if necessary.

| like – listen   dislike – take out   don't mind – clean   enjoy – do   like – watch   hate – pay |

1. Nina _____*likes*_____ _____*listening*_____ to music.

2. Erin _____ _____ homework.

3. Ahmad _____ _____ movies.

4. Yolanda and Sam _____ _____ bills.

5. Trudy _____ _____ the garbage.

6. Alma and Lara _____ _____ the house.

C Write questions using the verbs in parentheses. Write short answers. Add a sentence.

1. Nina likes swimming.

   (like) _Does Nina like swimming_ ? _Yes, she does. She likes swimming in the pool._

2. Ahmad loves dancing.

   (love) _____ ? _____

3. Yolanda and Sam hate shopping.

   (hate) _____ ? _____

4. Trudy doesn't mind cleaning.

   (mind) _____ ? _____

5. Alma and Lara enjoy playing cards.

   (dislike) _____ ? _____

D Write three questions to ask a classmate. Use *like*, *dislike*, *enjoy*, or *mind*.
Use the back of this paper.

Lesson C Comparisons

A Look at the chart. Circle *True* or *False*.

	play cards	read	watch TV	socialize	cook
Martina	5	4	3	2	1
Ron	3	4	1	2	5
Frank	1	5	4	3	2
Key: 1 = activity you like most, 5 = activity you like least					

1. Martina likes watching TV more than playing cards. (True) False
2. Martina enjoys socializing more than cooking. True False
3. Ron likes reading less than watching TV. True False
4. Ron enjoys socializing as much as Martina does. True False
5. Frank likes cooking less than playing cards. True False
6. Frank enjoys watching TV more than socializing. True False

B Complete the chart with information about you. Then complete the sentences.

Example: I like ___*dancing*___ more than ___*cooking*___ .

cooking	dancing	eating	shopping	watching TV

Number	Activity
1 (most)	
2	
3	
4	
5 (least)	

What do you like doing?

I like _____ more than _____ .

I like _____ less than _____ .

I like _____ more than _____ .

I like _____ less than _____ .

A Look at the chart. Circle the correct answers.

	play cards	read	watch TV	socialize	cook
Martina	5	4	3	2	1
Ron	3	4	1	2	5
Frank	1	5	4	3	2
Key: 1 = activity you like most, 5 = activity you like least					

1. Martina likes watching TV more than (**playing cards**)/ **socializing**.

2. Martina enjoys socializing less than **cooking / reading**.

3. Ron likes reading less than **cooking / watching TV**.

4. Ron enjoys socializing as much as **Frank does / Martina does**.

5. Frank likes cooking less than **socializing / playing cards**.

6. Frank enjoys watching TV less than **reading / socializing**.

B Complete the chart with information about you. Then complete the sentences.

Example: I like _dancing more than cooking_ .

cooking	dancing	eating	shopping	watching TV

Number	Activity
1 (most)	
2	
3	
4	
5 (least)	

What do you like doing?

(more) I like _____ .

(less) I like _____ .

(more) I like _____ .

(less) I like _____ .

Name: _____

Lesson C *Comparisons*

A Look at the chart. Complete the sentences. Use *more than*, *as much as*, or *less than*.

	play cards	read	watch TV	socialize	cook
Martina	5	4	3	2	1
Ron	3	4	1	2	5
Frank	1	5	4	3	2
Key: 1 = activity you like most, 5 = activity you like least					

1. Martina likes watching TV ____*more than*____ playing cards.

2. Martina enjoys socializing _____ cooking.

3. Ron likes reading _____ watching TV.

4. Ron enjoys socializing _____ Martina does.

5. Frank likes cooking _____ playing cards.

6. Frank enjoys watching TV _____ socializing.

B Complete the chart with information about you. Then write sentences. Use *more than* or *less than*.

Example: _*I like dancing more than cooking.*_____

cooking	dancing	eating	shopping	watching TV

Number	Activity
1 (most)	
2	
3	
4	
5 (least)	

What do you like doing?

_____

_____

_____

_____

Name: _____

Lesson D Reading

A Write the words in the correct column.

architect	friendly	nurse	scientist	think
creative	imagine	quiet	talk	

Jobs (nouns)	Personality (adjectives)	Activities (verbs)
architect	friendly	think

B Read the title. What is the topic of the article? Circle the correct answer.

a. the right personality   b. the right job   c. the right personality for the job

The Right Kind of Person for the Job

Gladys is a nurse. She is friendly and outgoing. She likes meeting new people. She gets along well with the nurses and patients. She enjoys talking to them.

Phuong is a scientist. She enjoys thinking about hard questions. She likes reading and she doesn't mind working alone. She is quiet and shy.

Benito is a musician. He likes playing music with his friends. He is creative. He loves writing new songs. His songs are different and interesting.

C Read the article in Exercise B. Then match.

1. Gladys likes __e__   a. nurses and patients.

2. Gladys enjoys talking to ____   b. reading.

3. Phuong enjoys thinking about ____   c. new songs.

4. Phuong likes ____   d. his friends.

5. Benito loves writing ____   e. meeting new people.

6. Benito likes playing music with ____   f. hard questions.

D Complete the sentences with information about you.

Example: _I am creative._

1. (personality) I am _____ .

2. (activities) I like _____ .

Name: _____

Lesson D *Reading*

A Write the words in the correct column.

architect	dancer	imagine	nurse	scientist	talk
creative	friendly	meet	quiet	shy	think

Jobs (nouns)		Personality (adjectives)		Activities (verbs)	
architect					

B Read the title. What is the topic of the article? Circle the correct answer.

a. the right personality   b. the right job   c. the right personality for the job

---

The Right Kind of Person for the Job

Gladys is a nurse. She is friendly and outgoing. She likes meeting new people. She gets along well with the nurses and patients. She enjoys talking to them.

Phuong is a scientist. She enjoys thinking about hard questions. She likes reading and she doesn't mind working alone. She is quiet and shy.

Benito is a musician. He likes playing music with his friends. He is creative. He loves writing new songs. His songs are different and interesting.

C Read the article in Exercise B. Then answer the questions.

1. What does Gladys like doing? _Meeting new people._____

2. Who does Gladys enjoy talking to? _____

3. What does Phuong enjoy thinking about? _____

4. What does Phuong like doing? _____

5. What does Benito love writing? _____

6. Who does Benito like playing music with? _____

D Complete the sentences with information about you.

Example: _I am creative and friendly._____

1. (personality) I am _____ and _____ .

2. (activities) I like _____ and _____ .

Name: _____

Lesson D Reading

A Write the words in the correct column. Add one more word in each column.
Use your dictionary if necessary.

architect	designer	imagine	outgoing	shy
creative	enjoy	meet	quiet	talk
dancer	friendly	nurse	scientist	think

Jobs (nouns)		Personality (adjectives)		Activities (verbs)	
architect					

B Read the title. What is the topic of the article? Circle the correct answer.

a. the right personality   b. the right job   c. the right personality for the job

The Right Kind of Person for the Job

Gladys is a nurse. She is friendly and outgoing. She likes meeting new people. She gets along well with the nurses and patients. She enjoys talking to them.

Phuong is a scientist. She enjoys thinking about hard questions. She likes reading and she doesn't mind working alone. She is quiet and shy.

Benito is a musician. He likes playing music with his friends. He is creative. He loves writing new songs. His songs are different and interesting.

C Read the article in Exercise B. Then write questions.

1. (What / do) _What does Gladys like doing_____? Meeting new people.

2. (Who / talk) _____? Nurses and patients.

3. (What / think) _____? Hard questions.

4. (What / do) _____? Reading.

5. (What / write) _____? New songs.

6. (Who / play music) _____? His friends.

D Complete the sentences with information about you.

I am _____ and _____ . I'm not _____ .

I like _____ . I don't like _____ .

Lesson E *Writing*

A Read the job ad. Answer the questions.

Counselor needed
at Los Altos Community Center

Do you have the right personality to
be a counselor? Are you outgoing and
friendly? Do you like talking to people
and helping them with their problems?
Contact us immediately. We have a job
for you.

1. What kind of job is this ad for? *A counselor.* _____

2. What kind of personality do you need? _____

3. What do you need to enjoy doing? _____

B Read about Eduardo. Complete the paragraph with words from the box.

counselor	helping	outgoing	personality	talking	work

   I think I have the right job for my personality. I'm a ___*counselor*___ .

I _____ in a community center in Los Altos. I am a very

_____ person. I like _____ to people. I am friendly. I enjoy

_____ people with their problems. I think a counselor is a good job

for me because it fits my _____ .

C Write about Eduardo. Use the information in Exercise B.

   Eduardo has the right job for his personality. He *is a counselor* . He

_____ in a community center in Los Altos. He _____

_____ _____ _____ person. He _____

_____ to people. He _____ _____ . He

_____ _____ people with their problems. He thinks a

counselor is a good job for _____ because it fits _____

_____ .

Name: _____

Lesson E *Writing*

A Read the job ad. Answer the questions.

> **Counselor needed**
> ### at Los Altos Community Center
> Do you have the right personality to be a counselor? Are you outgoing and friendly? Do you like talking to people and helping them with their problems? Contact us immediately. We have a job for you.

1. What kind of job is this ad for? *A counselor.* _____

2. What kind of personality do you need? _____

3. What do you need to enjoy doing? _____

4. Add two more ideas about the right personality for this job.

   A counselor is _____ .

   A counselor enjoys _____ .

B Read about Eduardo. Complete the paragraph. Use words from the ad in Exercise A.

I think I have the right job for my personality. I'm a ___*counselor*___ . I work in a community center in Los Altos. I am a very _____ person. I like _____ to people. I am friendly. I enjoy _____ people with their problems. I think a counselor is a good job for me because it fits my _____ .

C Write about Eduardo. Use the information in Exercise B.

Eduardo has the right job for his personality. He *is a counselor* . He _____ in a community center in Los Altos. He _____ person. He _____ to people. He _____ . He _____ people with their problems. He thinks a counselor is a good job for _____ because _____ .

14   **Add Ventures 3**   © Cambridge University Press 2008 **Photocopiable**

Lesson E Writing

A Read the job ad. Answer the questions.

> **Counselor needed**
> **at Los Altos Community Center**
>
> Do you have the right personality to be a counselor? Are you outgoing and friendly? Do you like talking to people and helping them with their problems? Contact us immediately. We have a job for you.

1. What kind of job is this ad for? _A counselor._ _____

2. What kind of personality do you need? _____

3. What do you need to enjoy doing? _____

4. Add some more ideas about the right personality for this job.

   A counselor is _____ and _____ .

   A counselor enjoys _____ and _____ .

B Read about Eduardo. Complete the paragraph. Use words from the ad in Exercise A.

   I think I have the right job for my personality. I'm a _counselor_ .
I work in a _____ in Los Altos. I am a very
_____ person. I like _____ to people. I am
friendly. I enjoy _____ people with _____ .
I think a counselor is a good job for me because it fits my
_____ .

C Write a paragraph about Eduardo. Use the information in Exercise B.

   Eduardo has the right job for his personality. He is a counselor.
He works _____

_____

_____

_____

_____

Add Ventures 3   **15**

Name: _____

Lesson F *Another view*

A Match the pictures with the correct descriptions below. Write the number.

| DM (42, 6'4") | DF (30, 5'0") | SM (20, 6'0") | SF (25, 5'8") |

☐   ☐   ☐   ☐

Enjoys running

Likes listening to music

Likes reading

Loves painting

Loves playing guitar

Enjoys gardening

Likes riding a motorcycle

Likes camping

B Circle *True* or *False*.

1. The shorter woman enjoys gardening.   (True)   False

2. The younger man hates running.   True   False

3. The older man likes playing guitar.   True   False

4. The taller woman loves painting.   True   False

5. The shorter woman loves camping.   True   False

C Complete the sentences about you.

1. I love _____ .

2. I like _____ .

3. I enjoy _____ .

4. I dislike _____ .

5. I am _____ .

Name: _____

Lesson F *Another view*

A Write the phrases under the correct pictures.

Loves playing guitar	Likes riding a motorcycle	Likes camping
Enjoys running	Likes reading	Loves painting
Likes listening to music	Enjoys gardening	

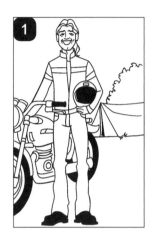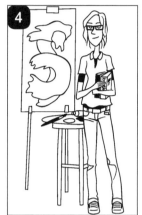

DM (42, 6'4")	**DF (30, 5'0")**	**SM (20, 6'0")**	**SF (25, 5'8")**
Likes riding a	_____	_____	_____
motorcycle	_____	_____	_____
_____	_____	_____	_____
_____	_____	_____	_____

B Match.

1. The shorter woman enjoys _d_   a. running.

2. The younger man enjoys ____   b. camping.

3. The older man likes ____   c. playing guitar.

4. The taller woman loves ____   d. gardening.

5. The shorter woman loves ____   e. painting.

C Complete the sentences about you and a friend.

I love _____ .   My friend loves _____ .

I enjoy _____ .   My friend enjoys _____ .

I dislike _____ .   My friend dislikes _____ .

I am _____ .   My friend is _____ .

Name: _____

Lesson F *Another view*

A Write phrases under the pictures. What do these people like doing?

DM (42, 6'4")	DF (30, 5'0")	SM (20, 6'0")	SF (25, 5'8")

Likes _r_____   Loves _p_____   Enjoys _r_____   Likes _r_____

_____   _____   Likes _l_____   Loves _p_____

Likes _c_____   Enjoys _g_____   _____

B Circle the correct answers.

1. Who enjoys gardening?   the taller woman / (the shorter woman)

2. Who enjoys running?   the older man / the younger man

3. Who likes camping?   the older man / the younger man

4. Who loves painting?   the taller woman / the shorter woman

5. Who loves playing guitar?   the older man / the shorter woman

C Complete the chart about you and your friend.

	You	**Your friend**	**Both**
1. activities you love			
2. activities you dislike			
3. your personality			

D Write about you and a friend. Use the chart in Exercise C. Use the back of this paper.

Example: *I love swimming. My friend loves running. We both love soccer.*

Lesson **A** *Get ready*

☑ ■ ■

A Match the problems and the advice.

1. I can't speak English well. __*b*__   a. Go to bed early.

2. I can't pronounce English words. ____   b. Talk to your classmates.

3. I can't remember vocabulary. ____   c. Study in a quiet room.

4. I can't concentrate. ____   d. Make a list of tasks.

5. I have too many things to do. ____   e. Listen carefully and repeat.

6. I'm always late for school. ____   f. Write new words on index cards.

B Complete the conversation.

Hi, Debbie. How's your English class?	Try to underline the main ideas.
You should write new words on index cards.	Don't feel discouraged. Make a list of tasks.
Maybe you need to study in a quiet place.	

Angela _Hi, Debbie. How's your English class?_
                                    (1)

Debbie Not so good. I have too many things to do.

Angela _____
                                    (2)

Debbie A list is a good idea. It's hard to remember everything. I can't concentrate.

Angela _____
                                    (3)

Debbie Yeah, maybe the library. And I can't remember all these new words.

Angela _____
                                    (4)

Debbie Yes, I should do that. This book is so boring, and I don't
                understand it.

Angela Be more active when you read.

_____
                                    (5)

Debbie I'll try that. Thanks for your advice.

Lesson **A** *Get ready*

A Complete the advice. Use the words in the box.

go	listen	make	study	talk	write

1. I can't speak English well.   *Talk*_____ to your classmates.

2. I can't pronounce English words.   _____ carefully and repeat.

3. I can't remember vocabulary.   _____ new words on index cards.

4. I can't concentrate.   _____ in a quiet room.

5. I have too many things to do.   _____ a list of tasks.

6. I'm always late for school.   _____ to bed early.

B Complete the conversation. Use the words in the box.

active	concentrate	English class	list	remember
boring	discouraged	index cards	quiet	underline

Angela Hi, Debbie. How's your *English class* ?
                                  (1)

Debbie Not so good. I have too many things to do.

Angela Don't feel _____ . Make a _____ of tasks.
                        (2)   (3)

Debbie A list is a good idea. It's hard to remember everything. I can't _____ .
                                                                            (4)

Angela Maybe you need to study in a _____ place.
                                          (5)

Debbie Yeah, maybe the library. And I can't _____ all these new words.
                                                 (6)

Angela You should write new words on _____ .
                                           (7)

Debbie Yes, I should do that. This book is so _____ , and I don't understand it.
                                                   (8)

Angela Be more _____ when you read. Try to _____ the main ideas.
                     (9)   (10)

Debbie I'll try that. Thanks for your advice.

Lesson A Get ready

A Complete the advice. Use the verbs in the box. Use some verbs twice.

ask	do	get	go	listen	make	study	talk	write

1. I can't speak English well.

   Talk to your classmates. _____ questions in class.

2. I can't pronounce English words.

   _____ carefully and repeat. _____ to a pronunciation CD.

3. I can't remember vocabulary.

   _____ new words on index cards. _____ new words in your notebook.

4. I can't concentrate.

   _____ in a quiet room. _____ in the library.

5. I have too many things to do.

   _____ a list of tasks. _____ important things first.

6. I'm always late for school.

   _____ to bed early. _____ up early.

B Complete the conversation with the words in the box. Add words if necessary.

a list of tasks	English class	index cards	a quiet place	underline

Angela Hi Debbie. How's _your English class_ _____ ?
                                              (1)

Debbie Not so good. I have too many things to do.

Angela Don't feel discouraged. Make _____ .
                                                        (2)

Debbie A list is a good idea. It's hard to remember everything. I can't concentrate.

Angela Maybe you need to study _____ .
                                                 (3)

Debbie Yeah, maybe the library. And I can't remember all these new words.

Angela You should write _____ .
                                         (4)

Debbie Yes, I should do that. This book is so boring, and I don't understand it.

Angela Be more active when you read. Try to _____ .
                                                            (5)

Debbie I'll try that. Thanks for your advice.

Lesson B *Present perfect*

Name: _____

A Complete the chart. Write the past participles of the verbs.

| be | know | live | speak | study | talk | teach | work |

Regular verbs (add *d* or *ed*, change *y* to *i* if needed)	**Irregular verbs**
1. *lived*	1. *been*
2.	2.
3.	3.
4.	4.

B Read the time line. Complete the sentences.

Julie's Recent History

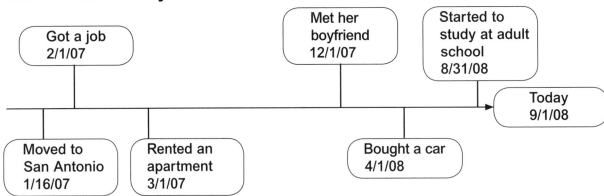

1. Julie has worked since *Feb. 1, 2007* .

2. She has lived in San Antonio since _____ .

3. She has lived in her apartment for _____ .

4. She has had her car for _____ .

5. She has known her boyfriend since _____ .

6. She has studied at the adult school for _____ .

C Write questions to ask your teacher.

1. (teach English) How long *have you taught English* ?

2. (live in this town) How long _____ ?

3. (be in class today) How long _____ ?

Lesson B *Present perfect*

A Complete the chart. Write the past participles of the verbs.

be	know	speak	talk	want
have	live	study	teach	work

Regular verbs		Irregular verbs	
1. *lived*	4.	1. *been*	4.
2.	5.	2.	5.
3.		3.	

B Read the time line. Complete the sentences.

Julie's Recent History

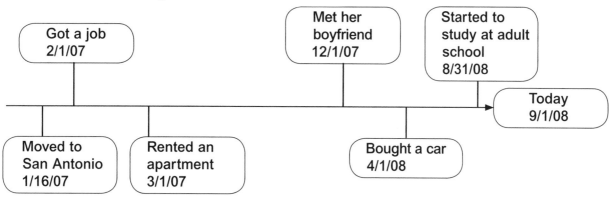

1. Julie has worked since _Feb. 1, 2007_____ .

2. She has lived in San Antonio since _____ .

3. She has lived in her apartment _____ one year and six months.

4. She has had her car for _____ .

5. She has known her boyfriend _____ Dec. 1, 2007.

6. She has studied at the adult school for _____ .

C Write questions to ask your teacher.

1. (teach English) How long _have you taught English_____ ?

2. (live in this town) How long _____ ?

3. (be in class today) How long _____ ?

4. (work at this school) How long _____ ?

Lesson B *Present perfect*

A Complete the charts. Write the past participles of the verbs. Label each group of verbs *Regular* or *Irregular*.

be	have	live	speak	talk	want
do	know	move	study	teach	work

_____ verbs	
1. *lived*	4.
2.	5.
3.	6.

_____ verbs	
1. *been*	4.
2.	5.
3.	6.

B Read the time line. Complete the sentences. Use the verbs in parentheses.

Julie's Recent History

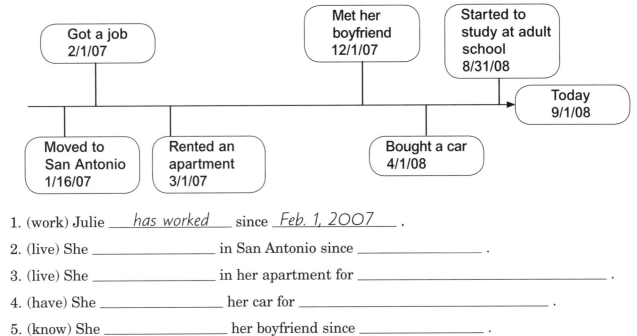

1. (work) Julie _____*has worked*_____ since ___*Feb. 1, 2007*___ .

2. (live) She _____ in San Antonio since _____ .

3. (live) She _____ in her apartment for _____ .

4. (have) She _____ her car for _____ .

5. (know) She _____ her boyfriend since _____ .

6. (study) She _____ at the adult school for _____ .

C Write questions to ask your teacher. Use the words in the box and *How long*? Use the back of this paper.

teach English   live in this town   be in class today   work at this school

Example: ___*How long have you taught English?*___

Lesson **C** *Present perfect*

A Complete the chart. Write the past participles of the verbs.

| ask | do | forget | make | study | try | underline | write |

Regular verbs (add *d* or *ed*, change *y* to *i* if needed)		**Irregular verbs**	
1. *asked*	3.	1. *did*	3.
2.	4.	2.	4.

B Complete the sentences with the past participle of the verbs in parentheses. Then answer the questions.

1. **A** Have you ever ____*asked*____ for more homework?
     (ask)

   B No, I ____*haven't*____ .

2. **A** Have they ever _____ late for school?
     (be)

   B No, they _____ .

3. **A** Has Marta ever _____ in class?
     (speak)

   B Yes, she _____ .

4. **A** Has Peter ever _____ the wrong homework?
     (do)

   B Yes, he _____ .

5. **A** Has your teacher ever _____ your name?
     (forget)

   B No, she _____ .

6. **A** Have you ever _____ a book in English?
     (read)

   B Yes, I _____ .

C Correct the sentences. Add the missing word.

1. Have ^*you* ever studied math?   (you)

2. she ever been to adult school?   (has)

3. Have they ever to the teacher?   (talked)

4. Has ever been late to school?   (he)

5. you ever forgotten your homework?   (have)

6. Has she ever the wrong bus?   (taken)

Name: _____

Lesson C *Present perfect*

A Complete the chart. Write the past participles of the verbs.

ask	do	forget	make	read	study	talk	try	underline	write

Regular verbs		Irregular verbs	
1. *asked*	4.	1. *did*	4.
2.	5.	2.	5.
3.		3.	

B Complete the sentences with the past participle of the verbs in the box.
Then answer the questions.

ask	be	do	forget	read	speak

1. **A** Have you ever __*asked*__ for more homework?

   B No, __*I haven't*__ .

2. **A** Have they ever _____ late for school?

   B No, _____ .

3. **A** Has Marta ever _____ in class?

   B Yes, _____ .

4. **A** Has Peter ever _____ the wrong homework?

   B Yes, _____ .

5. **A** Has your teacher ever _____ your name?

   B No, _____ .

6. **A** Have you ever _____ a book in English?

   B Yes, _____ .

C Correct the sentences. Add the missing word.

has	have	he	taken	talked	you

1. Have ᵧₒᵤ ever studied math?

2. she ever been to adult school?

3. Have they ever to the teacher?

4. Has ever been late to school?

5. you ever forgotten your homework?

6. Has she ever the wrong bus?

Lesson C Present perfect

A Complete the chart. Write the past participles of the verbs. Add two more verbs to each group.

ask	do	lose	read	talk	underline
concentrate	forget	make	study	try	write

Regular verbs		Irregular verbs	
1. *asked*	5.	1. *did*	5.
2.	6.	2.	6.
3.	7.	3.	7.
4.	8.	4.	8.

B Complete the sentences with the present perfect of an appropriate verb. Then answer the questions.

1. **A** ____*Have*____ you ever ____*asked*____ for more homework?

   B No, _*I haven't*_ .

2. **A** _____ they ever _____ late for school?

   B No, _____ .

3. **A** _____ Marta ever _____ in class?

   B Yes, _____ .

4. **A** _____ Peter ever _____ the wrong homework?

   B Yes, _____ .

5. **A** _____ your teacher ever _____ your name?

   B No, _____ .

6. **A** _____ you ever _____ a book in English?

   B Yes, _____ .

C Correct the sentences if necessary. Add the missing word.

1. Have ʌ ever studied math? *you*

2. she ever been to adult school?

3. Have they ever talked to the teacher?

4. Has he ever late to school?

5. you ever forgotten your homework?

6. Has she ever the wrong bus?

Lesson D Reading

✓ ■ ■

A Read the article. Which three strategies does the reading describe? Check (✓) the boxes.

☐ Read every word   ☐ Set a goal for reading every day
☐ Talk about the story   ☐ Use a dictionary
☑ Guess the meaning of new words   ☐ Translate every word

Strategies for Reading

When you read in English, you don't always need to understand every word. One strategy for reading better is to guess the meaning of new words. For example, use clues such as pictures and titles to help you work out the meaning.

Another strategy to improve your reading is to set a goal for reading every day. For example, plan to read two newspaper articles every day. Or choose a book and plan to read five pages every day.

When you finish an article or a book, a good strategy is to talk about the story in your own words. For example, tell a friend or your teacher about it. You'll understand the story better by explaining it to someone else.

B What advice does the article give? Circle the correct answers.

1. The article suggests three strategies for _____ .
   a. learning vocabulary   (c.) improving reading skills
   b. doing homework   d. correcting grammar mistakes

2. When you read in English, you should _____ .
   a. use a dictionary   c. translate every word
   b. guess new words   d. read every word

3. To improve your reading skills, you could try to _____ .
   a. read a lot   c. choose a book
   b. set a date   d. read every day

4. When you talk about a book, it helps you to _____ .
   a. understand it   c. read it
   b. finish it   d. like it

C Internet task: Look up the key words *study skills*. Find one Web site that gives advice about how to study. Write the Web address and one piece of advice here. If you do not have access to the Internet, write your own ideas.

Web address	Advice

Lesson D Reading

A Read the article. Underline the strategies. Circle the examples.

Strategies for Reading

When you read in English, you don't always need to understand every word. One strategy for reading better is to <u>guess the meaning of new words</u>. For example, (use clues such as pictures and titles) to help you work out the meaning.

Another strategy to improve your reading is to set a goal for reading every day. For example, plan to read two newspaper articles every day. Or choose a book and plan to read five pages every day.

When you finish an article or a book, a good strategy is to talk about the story in your own words. For example, tell a friend or your teacher about it. You'll understand the story better by explaining it to someone else.

B What advice does the article give? Circle the correct answers.

1. The article suggests three strategies for _____ .
   a. learning vocabulary   (c.) improving reading skills
   b. guessing new words   d. understanding main ideas

2. When you read in English, you should _____ .
   a. use a dictionary   c. guess the examples
   b. guess new words   d. read every word

3. To improve your reading skills, you could try to _____ .
   a. read a lot   c. choose a book
   b. read magazines   d. read every day

4. When you talk about a book, it helps you to _____ .
   a. understand it   c. read it
   b. finish it   d. forget it

C Internet task: Look up the key words *study skills*. Find two Web sites that give advice about how to study. Write the Web addresses and two pieces of advice here. If you do not have access to the Internet, use your own ideas.

Web address	Advice

Name: _____

Lesson **D** *Reading*

A Read the article and complete the chart.

> ## Strategies for Reading
>
> When you read in English, you don't always need to understand every word. One strategy for reading better is to guess the meaning of new words. For example, use clues such as pictures and titles to help you work out the meaning.
>
> Another strategy to improve your reading is to set a goal for reading every day. For example, plan to read two newspaper articles every day. Or choose a book and plan to read five pages every day.
>
> When you finish an article or a book, a good strategy is to talk about the story in your own words. For example, tell a friend or your teacher about it. You'll understand the story better by explaining it to someone else.

Strategies	Examples
Guess the meaning of new words.	

B What advice does the article give? Circle the correct answers.

1. The article suggests three strategies for ____ .
   a. learning new words
   (c.) improving reading skills
   b. setting goals
   d. understanding main ideas

2. When you read in English, you should ____ .
   a. try to understand everything
   c. guess the examples
   b. guess new words
   d. read every word

3. To improve your reading skills, you could try to ____ .
   a. read a lot
   c. choose a bok
   b. read magazines
   d. read every day

4. When you talk about a book, it helps you to ____ .
   a. understand it
   c. read it
   b. finish it
   d. explain it

C Internet task: Look up the key words *study skills*. Find three Web sites that give advice about how to study. Write the Web addresses and one piece of advice from each Web site. If you do not have access to the Internet, use your own ideas. Use the back of this paper.

A Read the chart and complete the paragraph.

Strategies for Writing	
Strategy	**Example**
1. *Plan your ideas.*	*Use a chart or make a list.*
2. *Check your work carefully.*	*Underline mistakes in grammar.*

I have read about some useful strategies for improving my writing. One strategy is to
_____ *plan my ideas* _____ . For example, I can _____ .
Another strategy is to _____ . For example, I can _____
_____ . I can't wait to try these new strategies, because I
want to write English better.

B Number the sentences in the best order for a paragraph.

Strategies for Speaking English

_____ For example, I can talk to them about sports, TV, or the weather.

_____ For example, I can use five new words every day.

_____ Another strategy is to speak English more often with my neighbors
or co-workers.

_____ I can't wait to try these new strategies, because I want to speak
English better.

_1_ I have read about some useful strategies for speaking English.

_____ One strategy is to set a goal for using new words.

C Write a paragraph using the sentences in Exercise B.

Strategies for Speaking English

_____

_____

_____

_____

_____

_____

_____

Name:

A Read the chart. Add your own ideas. Then complete the paragraph.

Strategies for Writing	
Strategy	**Example**
1. *Plan your ideas.*	*Use a chart or make a list.*
2. *Check your work carefully.*	*Underline mistakes in grammar.*
3.	

     I have read about some useful strategies for improving my writing. One strategy is ___*to plan my ideas*___ . For example, I can _____ _____ . Another strategy is to _____ _____ . For example, I can _____ _____ . A third strategy is to _____ _____ . For example, I can _____ _____ . I can't wait to try these new strategies, because I want to write English better.

B Complete the chart with your own ideas for speaking English better.

Strategies for Speaking English	
Strategy	**Example**
1. *Set a goal for using new words.*	*Use five new words every day.*
2.	
3.	

C Use your ideas to write a paragraph.

Strategies for Speaking English

     I have read about some useful strategies for speaking English. _____

_____

_____

_____

_____

_____ I can't

wait to try these new strategies, because I want to speak English better.

A Complete the chart with your own ideas. Then complete the paragraph.

Strategies for Writing	
Strategy	Example
1. *Plan your ideas.*	*Use a chart or make a list.*
2. *Check your work carefully.*	*Underline mistakes in grammar.*
3.	

    I have read about some useful strategies for improving my writing. One strategy is __*to plan my ideas*__ . For example, I can _____ _____ . Another strategy is to _____ _____ . For example, _____ _____ . A third strategy is to _____ _____ . For example, _____ .

I can't wait to try these new strategies, because I want to write English better.

B Complete the chart with your own ideas for speaking English better.

Strategies for Speaking English	
Strategy	Example
1.	
2.	
3.	

C Write a paragraph using your ideas from Exercise B.

Strategies for Speaking English

_____

_____

_____

_____

_____

_____

_____

Name: _____

Lesson F *Another view*

A Read the clues. Complete the crossword puzzle.

Tips for Taking Tests

Clues

Down

1. Can you _____ the question?

2. Don't _____ too much time on one question.

4. Leave time to _____ all your answers at the end.

Across

3. The _____ will tell you what to do.

5. Answer the _____ questions first.

6. You should _____ the whole test before you begin.

B Write some advice for a new student on how to study English. Use the topics in parentheses.

Example: (vocabulary) *Buy a good dictionary.* _____

1. (vocabulary) _____

2. (reading) _____

3. (pronunciation) _____

Lesson F *Another view*

Name: _____

A Read the clues. Complete the crossword puzzle.

Tips for Taking Tests

Clues

Down

1. Can you _____ the question?

2. Don't _____ too much time on one question.

4. Leave time to _____ all your answers at the end.

Across

3. The _____ will tell you what to do.

5. Answer the _____ questions first.

6. You should _____ the whole test before you begin.

B Write some advice for a new student on how to study English. Use the topics in parentheses.

Example: (vocabulary) *Buy a good dictionary.* _____

1. (vocabulary) _____

2. (reading) _____

3. (pronunciation) _____

4. (listening) _____

Lesson F *Another view*

A Read the clues. Complete the crossword puzzle.

Tips for Taking Tests

Clues

Down

1. The opposite of *ask.*
2. The opposite of *save.*
4. The same meaning as *make sure.*

Across

3. *Circle the answers* is an example of one.
5. The opposite of *difficult.*
6. Read something quickly to get the main idea.

B Write some advice for a new student on how to study English. Use the topics in the box.

| vocabulary | reading | pronunciation | listening | writing |

Example: (vocabulary) *Buy a good dictionary.*

1. _____

2. _____

3. _____

4. _____

5. _____

Name: _____

Lesson **A** *Get ready*

A Circle the correct response.

1. I need a favor.

   (a.) Sure. What do you need?

   b. I can give you a favor.

2. I can't reach the light.

   a. You can borrow my ladder.

   b. Do you need a favor?

3. My smoke alarm is beeping.

   a. Complain to your neighbor.

   b. You need to buy a new battery.

4. I need quarters for the washing machine.

   a. Do you need some money?

   b. I can lend you two quarters.

B Complete the sentences. Use *borrow* or *lend*.

1. Ana borrowed a ladder from Maria.

   Maria _____*lent a ladder*_____ to Ana.

2. Oscar borrowed five dollars from Steve.

   Steve _____ to Oscar.

3. The teacher lent some books to my children.

   My children _____ from the teacher.

4. I lent a dictionary to Manuela.

   Manuela _____ from me.

5. We borrowed some trash bags from our neighbor.

   Our neighbor _____ to us.

6. You borrowed a battery from Lee-Hom.

   Lee-Hom _____ to you.

C Solve the math problems.

1. Pablo lent $25 to Junko. He lent $18 to Henrik, and he lent $5 to Ken. How much money did he have to start with?
Answer: $25 + $18 + $5 = *$48*

2. Luis borrowed $15 from Suzanna. He lent $5 to Andy and $6 to Raymond. How much money does Luis have left?
Answer: $15 − $5 = _____ − $6 = _____

3. Elena borrowed $170 from Sam. She borrowed $230 from Peter. She lent $200 to Klara. How much money does she have left?
Answer: $170 + $230 = _____ − $200 = _____

Lesson **A** *Get ready*

A Match.

1. I need a favor. __c__

2. I can't reach the light. _____

3. My smoke alarm is beeping. _____

4. I need quarters for the washing machine. _____

a. I can lend you two quarters.

b. You need to buy a new battery.

c. Sure. What do you need?

d. You can borrow my ladder.

B Complete the sentences. Use *borrow* or *lend*.

1. Ana borrowed a ladder from Maria.

   Maria _lent a ladder to Ana_ .

2. Oscar borrowed five dollars from Steve.

   Steve _____ .

3. The teacher lent some books to my children.

   My children _____ .

4. I lent a dictionary to Manuela.

   Manuela _____ .

5. We borrowed some trash bags from our neighbor.

   Our neighbor _____ .

6. You borrowed a battery from Lee-Hom.

   Lee-Hom _____ .

C Solve the math problems.

1. Pablo lent $25 to Junko. He lent $18 to Henrik and $5 to Ken. How much money did he have to start with?
   Answer: ____$48____

2. Luis borrowed $15 from Suzanna. He lent $5 to Andy and $6 to Raymond. How much money does Luis have left?
   Answer: _____

3. Elena borrowed $170 from Sam. She borrowed $230 from Peter. She lent $200 to Klara. How much money does she have left?
   Answer: _____

Lesson A *Get ready*

A Write a response. Use the words in the box. Add words if necessary.

| borrow buy lend my ladder need new battery two quarters |

1. **A** I need a favor.
   B *Sure. What do you need?*

2. **A** I can't reach the light.
   B You can _____ .

3. **A** My smoke alarm is beeping.
   B You need _____ .

4. **A** I need quarters for the washing machine.
   B I can _____ .

B Write sentences with the same meaning. Use *borrow* or *lend*.

1. Ana borrowed a ladder from Maria.
   Maria lent a ladder to Ana.

2. Oscar borrowed five dollars from Steve.
   _____

3. The teacher lent some books to my children.
   _____

4. I lent a dictionary to Manuela.
   _____

5. We borrowed some trash bags from our neighbor.
   _____

6. You borrowed a battery from Lee-Hom.
   _____

C Solve the math problems. Write one more problem.

1. Pablo lent $25 to Junko. He lent $18 to Henrik and $5 to Ken. How much money did he have to start with?
   Answer: _____ *$48* _____

2. Luis borrowed $15 from Suzanna. He lent $5 to Andy and $6 to Raymond. How much money does Luis have left?
   Answer: _____

3. Elena borrowed $170 from Sam. She borrowed $230 from Peter. She lent $200 to Klara. How much money does she have left?
   Answer: _____

4. _____
   _____
   Answer: _____

Lesson B **Because** *and* **because of**

A Complete the sentences. Use *because* or *because of*.

1. Juan was late for work *because of* the traffic.

2. They couldn't play soccer _____ it was raining.

3. Simone couldn't sleep _____ it was noisy.

4. Rosanna studied a lot _____ she had an exam.

5. There was no school today _____ the holiday.

6. The roads were closed _____ an accident.

B Correct the sentences if necessary. Add *of*.

1. I couldn't find my door key because͜the broken light.
                                         of

2. We took our raincoats and umbrellas because the weather was bad.

3. We like the Mexican restaurant because the food is spicy.

4. Jim baked a cake for his wife because her birthday.

5. Tina couldn't go to school today because she had a cold.

C Complete the sentences with information about you.

1. I like / don't like my birthday because _____ .

2. I sometimes feel tired because _____ .

3. I am sometimes late for school / work because of _____ .

D Complete the chart.

Have you ever . . .	Why?
. . . had trouble sleeping?	*Because there was too much noise.*
. . . forgotten your homework?	
. . . borrowed something from a neighbor?	

Lesson B Because *and* because of

A Complete the sentences. Use *because* or *because of* and the phrases in the box.

an accident	it was raining	the holiday
it was noisy	she had an exam	the traffic

1. Juan was late for work *because of the traffic* _____ .

2. They couldn't play soccer _____ .

3. Simone couldn't sleep _____ .

4. Rosanna studied a lot _____ .

5. There was no school today _____ .

6. The roads were closed _____ .

B Correct the mistake in each sentence.

1. I couldn't find my door key because ^of the broken light.

2. We took our raincoats and umbrellas because the weather it was bad.

3. We like the Mexican restaurant because of the food is spicy.

4. Jim baked a cake for his wife because her birthday.

5. Tina couldn't go to school today because had a cold.

C Complete the sentences with information about you. Add one more sentence.

1. I like / don't like my birthday because _____ .

2. I sometimes feel tired because _____ .

3. I am sometimes late for school / work because of _____ .

4. _____ .

D Complete the chart. Add one more idea.

Have you ever . . .	Why?
. . . had trouble sleeping?	*Because there was too much noise.*
. . . forgotten your homework?	
. . . borrowed something from a neighbor?	

Lesson B Because *and* because of

A Complete the sentences. Use the words in parentheses.

1. Juan was late for work because of *the traffic* _____ . (traffic)
2. They couldn't play soccer because _____ . (rain)
3. Simone couldn't sleep because _____ . (noisy)
4. Rosanna studied a lot because _____ . (exam)
5. There was no school today because of _____ . (holiday)
6. The roads were closed because of _____ . (accident)

B Rewrite each sentence so that it has the same meaning. Use *because* or *because of*.

1. I couldn't find my door key because the light was broken.

   I couldn't find my door key because of the broken light. _____

2. They took their raincoats and umbrellas because of the bad weather.

   _____

3. We like the Mexican restaurant because of the spicy food.

   _____

4. Jim baked a cake for his wife because it was her birthday.

   _____

5. Tina couldn't go to school today because of her cold.

   _____

C Complete the sentences. Use *because* or *because of*. Add one more sentence.

1. I like / don't like my birthday _____ .
2. I sometimes feel tired _____ .
3. I am sometimes late for school / work _____ .
4. _____

D Complete the chart. Add two more ideas. Use the back of this paper.

Have you ever . . .	Why?
. . . had trouble sleeping?	*Because there was too much noise.*
. . . forgotten your homework?	
. . . borrowed something from a neighbor?	

Lesson C Enough *and* too

☑ ▓ ☐ 43

A Complete the sentences. Use *too* or *enough*.

1. I don't have time to bake a cake. I'm _____*too*_____ busy.

2. I have trouble concentrating here. It's _____ noisy.

3. You need to wash those dishes again. They're not clean _____ .

4. The exam started ten minutes ago. You're _____ late.

5. I don't like parties. I'm not outgoing _____ .

6. My children watch TV every day. They're not active _____ .

7. I can't buy a new TV. It's _____ expensive.

8. You should check your work again. You're not careful _____ .

B Correct the sentences. Add the missing word in parentheses.

1. The weather is cold today. It's ᴧcold to have a picnic.   (too)
   too

2. My son is 12 years old. He's not old to drive.   (enough)

3. The train left ten minutes ago. You're late.   (too)

4. I sit at my desk all day. I'm active enough.   (not)

5. The house has four bedrooms. It's large for the whole family.   (enough)

6. I often make mistakes. I'm careful enough.   (not)

C Which of these things do you dislike? Write two sentences. Use *too* and *not . . . enough*.

cell phones	English grammar	restaurants
dance clubs	Hollywood movies	shopping malls

Example: *I dislike shopping malls because they are too large. They're not friendly enough.*

1. _____

   _____

2. _____

   _____

Lesson **C** Enough *and* too

A Complete the sentences. Add *too* or *enough* and an adjective in the box.

active	careful	expensive	noisy
busy	clean	late	outgoing

1. I don't have time to bake a cake. I'm _too busy_____ .

2. I have trouble concentrating here. It's _____ .

3. You need to wash those dishes again. They're not _____ .

4. The exam started ten minutes ago. You're _____ .

5. I don't like parties. I'm not _____ .

6. My children watch TV every day. They're not _____ .

7. I can't buy a new TV. It's _____ .

8. You should check your work again. You're not _____ .

B Correct the sentences. Add *too, not,* or *enough*.

1. The weather is cold today. It's ∧cold to have a picnic.
   too

2. My son is 12 years old. He's not old to drive.

3. The train left ten minutes ago. You're late.

4. I sit at my desk all day. I'm active enough.

5. The house has four bedrooms. It's large for the whole family.

6. I often make mistakes. I'm careful enough.

C Which of these things do you dislike? Write two sentences. Use *too* and *not . . . enough*.

cell phones	English grammar	restaurants
dance clubs	Hollywood movies	shopping malls

Example: _I dislike shopping malls because they are too large. They're not friendly enough._

1. _____

   _____

2. _____

   _____

Lesson C Enough *and* too

A Complete the sentences. Add *too* or *not . . . enough* and an adjective in the box.

active	careful	expensive	noisy
busy	clean	late	outgoing

1. I don't have time to bake a cake. I'm _too busy_____ .

2. I have trouble concentrating here. It's _____ .

3. You need to wash those dishes again. They're _____ .

4. The exam started ten minutes ago. You're _____ .

5. I don't like parties. I'm _____ .

6. My children watch TV every day. They're _____ .

7. I can't buy a new TV. It's _____ .

8. You should check your work again. You're _____ .

B Correct the sentences. Add the missing word.

                                     too

1. The weather is cold today. It's∧cold to have a picnic.

2. My son is 12 years old. He's not old to drive.

3. The train left ten minutes ago. You're late.

4. I sit at my desk all day. I'm active enough.

5. The house has four bedrooms. It's large for the whole family.

6. I often make mistakes. I'm careful enough.

C Which of these things do you dislike? Write three sentences. Use *too* and *not . . . enough*. Add your own ideas.

cell phones	English grammar	restaurants
dance clubs	Hollywood movies	shopping malls

Example: *I dislike shopping malls because they are too large. They aren't friendly enough.*

1. _____

   _____

2. _____

   _____

3. _____

   _____

Lesson **D** *Reading*

A Read the article. Find two-word verbs with the same meaning.

1. escape *get away*

2. made a loud noise _____

3. take care of _____

4. entered illegally _____

5. meet _____

6. enter (a car) legally _____

A Helpful Neighbor

My alarm **went off** while I was away on vacation. Someone **broke into** my apartment. My neighbor heard the alarm and called 9-1-1. She looked out the kitchen window and saw a tall man in a dark jacket. He was trying to **get away** through the backyard. She described the man to the police. Later that night, the police arrested a man. He was carrying a large bag full of CDs and CD players and was about to **get into** a car.

I'm very glad that my neighbors **watch out for** each other. I feel safe in this neighborhood. I'm going to **get together** with my neighbor this weekend and take her out for dinner to say thank you for her help.

B Read the article again. Circle the correct answers.

1. The neighbor called the police because _____ .
   a. the writer was on vacation
   b. she looked out the kitchen window
   c. she heard the alarm

2. The neighbor told the police _____ .
   a. she saw a tall man in a dark jacket
   b. she didn't see the man
   c. she saw a man with a bag of CDs

3. The writer and the neighbor are going to _____ .
   a. get together with all her neighbors
   b. go out for dinner
   c. cook dinner together

4. The main idea of the article is:
   a. My alarm went off.
   b. The police arrested a man.
   c. My neighbors watch out for each other.

C How do you keep your neighborhood safe? Write two examples.

1. _____

_____

2. _____

_____

Lesson D Reading

A Read the article. Use the two-word verbs in the box to complete the sentences.

broke into	get away	get into	get together	watch out	went off

A Helpful Neighbor

My alarm ____*went off*____ while I was away on vacation. Someone
_____ my apartment. My neighbor heard the alarm and called 9-1-1.
2
She looked out the kitchen window and saw a tall man in a dark jacket. He was

trying to _____ through the backyard. She described the man to the
3
police. Later that night, the police arrested a man. He was carrying a large bag

full of CDs and CD players and was about to _____ a car.
4
    I'm very glad that my neighbors _____ for each other. I feel safe in
5
this neighborhood. I'm going to _____ with my neighbor this weekend
6
and take her out for dinner to say thank you for her help.

B Read the article again. Circle the correct answers.

1. The neighbor called the police
   because _____ .
   a. the writer was on vacation
   b. she saw a tall man
   c. she heard the alarm
   d. she looked out the kitchen window

2. The neighbor told the police _____ .
   a. she saw a tall man in a dark jacket
   b. she didn't see the man
   c. she saw a man in a car
   d. she saw a man with a bag of CDs

3. The writer and the neighbor are
   going to _____ .
   a. get together with all her neighbors
   b. go out for dinner
   c. cook dinner together
   d. get takeout

4. The main idea of the article is:
   a. My alarm went off.
   b. The police arrested a man.
   c. My neighbors watch out for each other.
   d. I'm going to thank my neighbor.

C How do you keep your neighborhood safe? Write two examples.

1. _____

_____

2. _____

_____

Lesson D *Reading*

A Read the article. Use the words in the box to make two-word verbs.

| broke | get | get | get | watch | went |

A Helpful Neighbor

My alarm _____went off_____ while I was away on vacation. Someone
          1
_____ my apartment. My neighbor heard the alarm and
          2
called 9-1-1. She looked out the kitchen window and saw a tall man in
a dark jacket. He was trying to _____ through the backyard.
                                          3
She described the man to the police. Later that night, the police
arrested a man. He was carying a large bag full of CDs and CD players
and was about to _____ a car.
                          4
I'm very glad that my neighbors _____ for each other. I
                                          5
feel safe in this neighborhood. I'm going to _____ with my
                                                        6
neighbor this weekend and take her out for dinner to say thank you for
her help.

B Read the article again. Answer the questions.

1. Why did the neighbor call the police?
   The neighbor called the police because she heard the alarm.

2. What did the neighbor tell the police?
   _____

3. What are the writer and the neighbor going to do?
   _____

4. What is the main idea of the article? Choose one.

   | My alarm went off. | My neighbors watch out for each other. |
   | The police arrested a man. | I am going to thank my neighbor. |

   The main idea of the article is: _____

C How do you keep your neighborhood safe? Write three examples. Use the
back of this paper.

 **Lesson E** *Writing*

A Match the problems with the requests.

1. My bathroom sink is leaking. __c__   a. Can you please clean it up?

2. There is garbage in the hallway. ____   b. Can you please put in a new light?

3. My door lock is broken. ____   c. Can you please send a repair person?

4. There is graffiti on the wall. ____   d. Can you please tell them to be quiet?

5. The neighbors are too noisy. ____   e. Can you please fix it?

6. The hallway is too dark. ____   f. Can you please paint over it?

B Number the sentences in the correct order for a letter of complaint.

____ To Whom It May Concern: ____ Greenway Properties
                                           267 South Street
__1__ December 21, 2007   Richmond, VA 23228

____ My bathroom sink is leaking.   ____ Sincerely,

____ Can you please send a repair person?

C Write the letter of complaint. Use the sentences from Exercise B.

_____

_____

_____

_____

_____ :

I live at 233 Central Avenue, Apt. 12.
_____
_____
Thank you in advance.

_____
Raymond D. Souza
Raymond D. Souza

Name: _____

Lesson **E** *Writing*

A Read the problems. Write a request for each problem. Use *Can you please . . . ?*

1. My bathroom sink is leaking.

   (send) *Can you please send a repair person?* _____

2. There is garbage in the hallway.

   (clean up) _____

3. My door lock is broken.

   (fix) _____

4. There is graffiti on the wall.

   (paint over) _____

5. The neighbors are too noisy.

   (tell) _____

6. The hallway is too dark.

   (put in) _____

B Number the sentences in the correct order for a letter of complaint.

   _____ To Whom It May Concern:

   _1_ December 21, 2007

   _____ Thank you in advance.

   _____ My bathroom sink is leaking.

   _____ Raymond D. Souza

   _____ I live at 233 Central Avenue, Apt. 12.

   _____ Greenway Properties
   267 South Street
   Richmond, VA 23228

   _____ Sincerely,

   _____ Can you please send a repair person?

C Write a letter of complaint on the back of this paper. Use the sentences
from Exercise B.

Lesson E *Writing*

A Read the problems. Write a request for each problem. Use *Can you please . . . ?*

1. My bathroom sink is leaking.

   Can you please send a repair person? _____

2. There is garbage in the hallway.

   _____

3. My door lock is broken.

   _____

4. There is graffiti on the wall.

   _____

5. The neighbors are too noisy.

   _____

6. The hallway is too dark.

   _____

B Number the sentences in the correct order for a letter of complaint.

_____ To Whom It May Concern:

__1__ December 21, 2007

_____ Thank you in advance.

_____ My bathroom sink is leaking.

_____ I live at 233 Central Avenue, Apt. 12.

_____ Greenway Properties
267 South Street
Richmond, VA 23228

_____ Sincerely,

_____ I hope you will take of care of this as
soon as possible.

_____ Can you please send a repair person?

_____ Raymond D. Souza

_____ Because of the leak, we are using too much water.

C Write the letter of complaint on the back of this paper. Use the sentences
from Exercise B.

Name: _____

Lesson F | *Another view*

A Look at the volunteer ad. Match Ludmila's questions and the librarian's answers.

 Library Volunteers Needed

Organization: Oak Park Public Library   **Location:** 3411 Green Avenue

Volunteers needed: 3

Date: Immediately   **Time:** Wed. and Fri. 3–6 p.m.

Description: Re-shelve books, help visitors to use the Internet

Requirements: Friendly personality, computer experience

Ludmila:

1. How many volunteers do you need? _b_

2. How many hours a week can we work? ____

3. What do the volunteers do? ____

4. What kind of experience do we need? ____

5. When can I start? ____

Librarian:

a. You can start immediately.

b. We need three volunteers.

c. You need to have computer experience.

d. You can work 6 hours a week.

e. They re-shelve books and help visitors to use the Internet.

B What kind of volunteer work can you do at these places? Circle the correct answers.

1. Neighborhood Fair   I can pick up trash. / (I can bake cookies.)

2. Food Bank   I can collect food. / I can take care of animals.

3. Animal Shelter   I can read stories to children. / I can take care of animals.

4. Neighborhood Clean-up   I can collect food. / I can pick up trash.

5. Children's Book Club   I can talk to seniors. / I can read stories to children.

6. Senior Care Center   I can bake cookies. / I can talk to seniors.

C Which volunteer work in Exercise B would you like to do? Tell why.

_____

_____

Lesson F *Another view*

A Look at the volunteer ad. Complete the conversation.

> **Library Volunteers Needed**
>
> **Organization:** Oak Park Public Library   **Location:** 3411 Green Avenue
> **Volunteers needed:** 3
> **Date:** Immediately   **Time:** Wed. and Fri. 3–6 p.m.
> **Description:** Re-shelve books, help visitors to use the Internet
> **Requirements:** Friendly personality, computer experience

1. ***Ludmila***   How many volunteers do you need?
   Librarian   We need ____*three*____ volunteers.

2. ***Ludmila***   How many hours a week can we work?
   Librarian   You can work _____ hours a week.

3. ***Ludmila***   What do the volunteers do?
   Librarian   They _____ .

4. ***Ludmila***   What kind of experience do we need?
   Librarian   You need to have _____ .

5. ***Ludmila***   When can I start?
   Librarian   You can start _____ .

B What kind of volunteer work can you do at these places? Match.

1. Neighborhood Fair __*f*__   a. I can pick up trash.
2. Food Bank ____   b. I can take care of animals.
3. Animal Shelter ____   c. I can read stories to children.
4. Neighborhood Clean-up ____   d. I can collect food.
5. Children's Book Club ____   e. I can talk to seniors.
6. Senior Care Center ____   f. I can bake cookies.

C Which volunteer work in Exercise B would you like to do? Tell why.

_____

_____

Lesson F Another view

A Look at the volunteer ad. Complete the conversation.

> ## 📚 Library Volunteers Needed
>
> **Organization:** Oak Park Public Library   **Location:** 3411 Green Avenue
> **Volunteers needed:** 3
> **Date:** Immediately   **Time:** Wed. and Fri. 3–6 p.m.
> **Description:** Re-shelve books, help visitors to use the Internet
> **Requirements:** Friendly personality, computer experience

1. **Ludmila** How many volunteers do you need?

   Librarian *We need three volunteers.*

2. **Ludmila** How many hours a week can we work?

   Librarian _____

3. **Ludmila** What do the volunteers do?

   Librarian _____

4. **Ludmila** What kind of experience do we need?

   Librarian _____

5. **Ludmila** When can I start?

   Librarian _____

B What kind of volunteer work can you do at these places? Write sentences.
Use the words in both boxes.

bake	pick up	take care of
collect	read	talk

animals	food	stories
cookies	seniors	trash

1. Neighborhood Fair: *I can bake cookies.* _____

2. Food Bank: _____

3. Animal Shelter: _____

4. Neighborhood Clean-up: _____

5. Children's Book Club: _____

6. Senior Care Center: _____

C Which volunteer work in Exercise B would you like to do? Tell why. Use the back of this paper.

Lesson A *Get ready*

A Put the sentences in the correct order to make a conversation.

_____ I see. What's the problem?

_1_ Hello, doctor. I'm worried about my health.

_____ Yes, I have. I think it's because I eat too much candy.

_____ Not really. I drive my car every day.

_____ Well, I get enough sleep, but I feel tired all day.

_____ That's possible. Do you get regular exercise?

_____ Maybe you're tired because you don't have a healthy diet. Have you gained weight?

_8_ Not enough exercise can also make you feel tired. Let's check your blood pressure now.

B Match the problems with the advice.

1. I feel tired all the time. _e_   a. You should talk to a doctor.

2. I sit at my desk all day. _____   b. You should eat more fruit and vegetables.

3. I want to have a healthy diet. _____   c. You should watch your diet.

4. I'm worried about my health. _____   d. You should get more exercise.

5. I eat too much candy. _____   e. You should get more sleep.

C Do you take care of your health? Write two questions. Then write your answers.

Example: *Do you ride a bicycle?*

No, I don't. But I take a walk every day.

1. (exercise) Do you _____ ?

_____

2. (food) Do you _____ ?

_____

Add Ventures 3   **55**

Lesson A Get ready

A Complete the conversation.

candy	check	diet	drive	exercise	health	problem	regular	tired	weight

Stan Hello, doctor. I'm worried about my ___*health*___ .
                                                          1

Doctor I see. What's the _____ ?
                                       2

Stan Well, I get enough sleep, but I feel _____ all day.
                                                          3

Doctor Maybe you're tired because you don't have a healthy _____ . Have you gained
                                                                          4

_____ ?
        5

Stan Yes, I have. I think it's because I eat too much _____ .
                                                                    6

Doctor That's possible. Do you get _____ exercise?
                                                  7

Stan Not really. I _____ my car every day.
                            8

Doctor Not enough _____ can also make you feel tired. Let's
                                9

_____ your blood pressure now.
      10

B Complete each piece of advice.

a doctor	diet	exercise	fruit and vegetables	sleep

1. **A** I feel tired all the time.

   B You should get more ___*sleep*___ .

2. **A** I sit at my desk all day.

   B You should get more _____ .

3. **A** I want to have a healthy diet.

   B You should eat more _____ .

4. **A** I'm worried about my health.

   B You should talk to _____ .

5. **A** I eat too much candy.

   B You should watch your _____ .

C Do you take care of your health? Write three questions. Then write
your answers.

Example: *Do you ride a bicycle?*   *No, I don't. But I take a walk every day.*

1. (exercise) Do you _____ ? _____

2. (food) Do you _____ ? _____

3. (see a doctor) Do you _____ ? _____

Lesson A Get ready

A Complete the conversation.

I feel tired all day	I'm worried about my health
you don't have a healthy diet	What's the problem
Let's check your blood pressure	I eat too much candy
regular exercise	I drive my car

Stan Hello, doctor. _I'm worried about my health_ .
1

Doctor I see. _____ ?
2

Stan Well, I get enough sleep, but _____ .
3

Doctor Maybe you're tired because _____ . Have you
4
gained weight?

Stan Yes, I have. I think it's because _____ .
5

Doctor That's possible. Do you get _____ ?
6

Stan Not really. _____ every day.
7

Doctor Not enough exercise can also make you feel tired.

_____ now.
8

B Write one piece of advice for each problem.

1. I feel tired all the time.   _You should get more sleep._

2. I sit at my desk all day.   _____

3. I want to have a healthy diet.   _____

4. I'm worried about my health.   _____

5. I eat too much candy.   _____

C Do you take care of your health? Write four questions. Then write
your answers.

Example: _Do you ride a bicycle?_   _No, I don't. But I take a walk every day._

1. (exercise) _____ ?   _____

2. (food) _____ ?   _____

3. (see a doctor) _____ ?   _____

4. (sleep) _____ ?   _____

Name: _____

Lesson B *Present perfect*

A Look at the chart. Write questions and answers.

What have they done recently?					
	go to the gym	lose weight	eat vegetables	visit the doctor	take vitamins
Osman	✓		✓	✓	✓
Lucia		✓	✓		
Alex				✓	✓
Eva	✓	✓			

1. (Osman / go) _Has Osman gone_____ to the gym recently?   Yes, he __has__ .

2. (Lucia / lose) _____ weight lately?   Yes, she _____ .

3. (Alex / eat) _____ vegetables lately?   No, he _____ .

4. (Osman and Alex / visit) _____ the doctor recently?

   Yes, they _____ .

5. (Lucia and Eva / take) _____ vitamins recently?

   No, they _____ .

B Complete the questions. Write answers about you.

1. (check) Have you __checked__ your blood pressure recently?   _Yes, I have._____

2. (visit) Have you _____ a dentist lately?   _____

3. (have) Have you _____ a cold recently?   _____

4. (take) Have you _____ vitamins recently?   _____

5. (play) Have you _____ soccer lately?   _____

6. (eat) Have you _____ fish recently?   _____

C Write two things you have done for your health recently. Use your own ideas.

Example: _I've given up desserts.____

1. _____

2. _____

Lesson B *Present perfect*

A Look at the chart. Write questions and answers.

What have they done (or not done) recently?					
	go to the gym	lose weight	eat vegetables	visit the doctor	take vitamins
Osman	✓		✓	✓	✓
Lucia		✓	✓		
Alex				✓	✓
Eva	✓	✓			

1. (Osman) _Has Osman gone_____ to the gym recently? _Yes, he has._____

2. (Lucia) _____ weight lately? _____

3. (Alex) _____ vegetables lately? _____

4. (Osman and Alex) _____ the doctor recently? _____

5. (Lucia and Eva) _____ vitamins recently? _____

B Complete the questions. Use the verbs in the box. Write answers about you. Add one more question and answer.

check   eat   have   play   take   visit

1. Have you ___checked___ your blood pressure recently? _Yes I have._____

2. Have you _____ a dentist lately? _____

3. Have you _____ a cold recently? _____

4. Have you _____ vitamins recently? _____

5. Have you _____ soccer lately? _____

6. Have you _____ fish recently? _____

7. Have you _____ recently? _____

C Write three things you have done for your health recently. Use your own ideas.

Example: _I've given up desserts._____

1. _____

2. _____

3. _____

Lesson B *Present perfect*

Name: _____

A Look at the chart. Write questions and answers.

What have they done (or not done) recently?	go to the gym	lose weight	eat vegetables	visit the doctor	take vitamins
Osman	✓		✓	✓	✓
Lucia		✓	✓		
Alex				✓	✓
Eva	✓	✓			

1. (Osman / gym) *Has Osman gone to the gym recently?*   *Yes, he has.*

2. (Lucia / weight) _____ ? _____

3. (Alex / vegetables) _____ ? _____

4. (Osman and Alex / doctor) _____ ? _____

5. (Lucia and Eva / vitamins) _____ ? _____

B Complete the questions. Use appropriate verbs. Write answers about you.
Add two more questions and answers.

1. *Have* you *checked* your blood pressure recently?   *Yes I have.*

2. _____ you _____ a dentist lately?   _____

3. _____ you _____ a cold recently?   _____

4. _____ you _____ vitamins recently?   _____

5. _____ you _____ soccer lately?   _____

6. _____ you _____ fish recently?   _____

7. _____ you _____ recently?   _____

8. _____ you _____ recently?   _____

C Write four things you have done for your health recently. Use your
own ideas.

Example: *I've given up desserts.*

1. _____

2. _____

3. _____

4. _____

Name: _____

Lesson C Used to

A Write sentences about before and now. Use *used to.*

1. play soccer / baseball

   Steve _used to play soccer_ , but now he

   plays baseball .

2. eat potato chips / fruit

   He _____ , but now he

   _____ .

3. drink soda / fruit juice

   Marta _____ , but now she

   _____ .

4. go to bed late / early

   She _____ , but now she

   _____ .

5. eat ice cream / yogurt

   Steve and Marta _____ , but now

   they _____ .

6. ride bikes / drive a car

   They _____ , but now they _____ .

10 Years Ago

Now

B Use the information in Exercise A to complete the questions and answers. Use *use to.*

1. Did Steve _use to play soccer_____ ?   Yes, he _did____ .
   (play soccer)

2. Did Steve _____ ?   No, he _____ .
   (eat fruit)

3. Did Marta _____ ?   No, she _____ .
   (drink fruit juice)

4. Did Marta _____ ?   Yes, she _____ .
   (go to bed late)

5. Did Steve and Marta _____ ?   Yes, they _____ .
   (eat ice cream)

6. Did Steve and Marta _____ ?   No, they _____ .
   (drive a car)

C Write a sentence about something you used to do.

_____ .

Lesson C Used to

A Write sentences about before and now. Use *used to*.

1. Steve / play soccer / baseball

   <u>Steve used to play soccer</u> , <u>but now he plays baseball.</u>

2. He / eat potato chips / fruit

   _____ , _____

3. Marta / drink soda / fruit juice

   _____ , _____

4. She / go to bed late / early

   _____ , _____

5. Steve and Marta / eat ice cream / yogurt

   _____ , _____

6. They / ride bikes / drive a car

   _____ , _____

10 Years Ago

Now

B Use the information in Exercise A to complete the questions and answers. Use *use to*.

1. Steve / play soccer

   <u>Did Steve use to play soccer</u> ? Yes, he <u>did</u> .

2. Steve / eat fruit

   _____ ? No, he _____ .

3. Marta / drink fruit juice

   _____ ? No, she _____ .

4. Marta / go to bed late

   _____ ? Yes, she _____ .

5. Steve and Marta / eat ice cream

   _____ ? Yes, they _____ .

6. Steve and Marta / drive a car

   _____ ? No, they _____ .

C Write two sentences about things you used to do.

_____ .

_____ .

Lesson **C** Used to

A Write sentences about before and now. Use *used to.*

1. Steve / soccer / baseball

   <u>Steve used to play soccer</u> , <u>but now he plays baseball.</u>

2. He / potato chips / fruit

   _____ , _____

3. Marta / soda / fruit juice

   _____ , _____

4. She / bed late / early

   _____ , _____

5. Steve and Marta / ice cream / yogurt

   _____ , _____

6. They / bikes / car

   _____ , _____

10 Years Ago

Now

B Use the information in Exercise A to complete the questions and answers. Use *use to.*

1. Steve / play soccer

   <u>Did Steve use to play soccer</u> ? <u>Yes, he did.</u>

2. Steve / eat fruit

   _____ ? _____

3. Marta / drink fruit juice

   _____ ? _____

4. Marta / go to bed late

   _____ ? _____

5. Steve and Marta / eat ice cream

   _____ ? _____

6. Steve and Marta / drive a car

   _____ ? _____

C Write three sentences about things you used to do.

_____ .

_____ .

_____ .

Lesson D *Reading*

A Look at the words in **bold**. Circle the correct part of speech.

1. Garlic can **prevent** high blood pressure. (verb) / noun / adjective

2. Chamomile tea helps your **digestion**. verb / noun / adjective

3. You can make an **herbal** tea from mint. verb / noun / adjective

4. Some people use garlic to **treat** insect bites. verb / noun / adjective

5. Colds and flu are two different **sicknesses**. verb / noun / adjective

B Read the article. Circle the correct answers.

Healthful Plants

Many people grow herbs in their garden or in their home. They use herbs for cooking and treating illnesses. Garlic and chamomile are two kinds of herbal plants, and they have many uses.

Some people use garlic to treat high blood pressure. You can use garlic in soup, fish, or meat. Garlic is a traditional treatment for insect bites as well.

Chamomile tea is a popular treatment for colds and flu. People with poor digestion sometimes drink chamomile tea after a meal. People with sleeping problems drink it before they go to bed.

Many people use herbs to prevent sickness because they are more natural than other types of medicine and they usually taste good.

---

1. You can use **garlic** / **chamomile** when you cook soup.

2. You can use **garlic** / **chamomile** to make tea.

3. You can use **garlic** / **chamomile** for high blood pressure.

4. You can use **garlic** / **chamomile** for colds and flu.

5. You can use **garlic** / **chamomile** to help digestion.

6. You can use **garlic** / **chamomile** to help you sleep.

C Internet task: Look up the key words *herbal plants*. Find the name of one herbal plant. If you do not have access to the Internet, write about an herbal plant you know. What illnesses can you use it for?

Name of plant: _____

Used to treat: _____

Lesson D Reading

A Complete the sentences with a word in the box. Then circle the correct part of speech.

| digestion | herbal | prevent | sicknesses | treat |

1. Garlic can ___*prevent*___ high blood pressure. (verb)/ noun / adjective

2. Chamomile tea helps your _____ . verb / noun / adjective

3. You can make an _____ tea from mint. verb / noun / adjective

4. Some people use garlic to _____ insect bites. verb / noun / adjective

5. Colds and flu are two different _____ . verb / noun / adjective

B Read the article. Complete the chart.

Healthful Plants

Many people grow herbs in their garden or in their home. They use herbs for cooking and treating illnesses. Garlic and chamomile are two kinds of herbal plants, and they have many uses.

Some people use garlic to treat high blood pressure. You can use garlic in soup, fish, or meat. Garlic is a traditional treatment for insect bites as well.

Chamomile tea is a popular treatment for colds and flu. People with poor digestion sometimes drink chamomile tea after a meal. People with sleeping problems drink it before they go to bed.

Many people use herbs to prevent sickness because they are more natural than other types of medicine and they usually taste good.

| when you cook soup | for colds and flu | to help you sleep | to make tea |
| for high blood pressure | to help digestion | for insect bites | with fish or meat |

You can use garlic:	You can use chamomile:
when you cook soup	*to make tea*

C Internet task: Look up the key words *herbal plants*. Find the names of two plants. If you do not have access to the Internet, write about herbal plants you know. What illnesses can you use them for? Use the back of this paper.

A Complete the sentences. Use the correct form of the words in the box.
Then circle the part of speech.

digest	herb	prevent	sick	treat

1. Garlic can ___*prevent*___ high blood pressure.　　　(verb)/ noun / adjective

2. Chamomile tea helps your _____ .　　　verb / noun / adjective

3. You can make an _____ tea from mint.　　　verb / noun / adjective

4. Some people use garlic to _____ insect bites.　　　verb / noun / adjective

5. Colds and flu are two different _____ .　　　verb / noun / adjective

B Read the article. Complete the chart.

Healthful Plants

　　Many people grow herbs in their garden or in their home. They use herbs for cooking and treating illnesses. Garlic and chamomile are two kinds of herbal plants, and they have many uses.

　　Some people use garlic to treat high blood pressure. You can use garlic in soup, fish, or meat. Garlic is a traditional treatment for insect bites as well.

　　Chamomile tea is a popular treatment for colds and flu. People with poor digestion sometimes drink chamomile tea after a meal. People with sleeping problems drink it before they go to bed.

　　Many people use herbs to prevent sickness because they are more natural than other types of medicine and they usually taste good.

You can use garlic:	You can use chamomile:
when you cook soup	*to make tea*

C Internet task: Look up the key words *herbal plants*. Find the name of three herbal plants. If you do not have access to the Internet, write about herbal plants you know. What illnesses can you use them for? Use the back of this paper.

A Complete the paragraph. Use the words in the box.

drank	has	has	helps	is	made	make	used

Mint ___*is*___ a popular herb in my country. The plant _____
   1   2

small dark green leaves. It _____ a fresh smell. We _____ to grow
                              3   4

mint in our garden when I was a child. We dried the leaves and _____
                                                                    5

tea from them. It _____ with indigestion and upset stomachs. We
                    6

usually _____ mint tea after every meal. Today, I _____ iced mint
          7   8

tea in the summer.

mint

B Read the paragraph in Exercise A again. Correct the sentences.

1. Mint is ~~not~~ a popular herb.

2. It has large dark green leaves.

3. The writer didn't grow mint in her garden.

4. The writer made tea from the flowers.

5. Mint tea is good for headaches.

6. The writer's family drank mint tea before every meal.

7. Today, the writer likes to make hot mint tea.

C Use the information in the chart to write a paragraph about lavender.

Name of plant	Appearance	Use dried flowers to . . .
Lavender	Silver-green leaves and tiny purple flowers	Make tea (good for headaches) Make bath oil (very relaxing)

_____ is a popular plant. It has _____ and

_____ . You can use the dried flowers to _____ .

It helps with _____ . You can also make _____ .

It is _____ .

Lesson E *Writing*

A Complete the paragraph. Use the words in the box.

child	herb	indigestion	leaves	meal	tea

Mint is a popular ____*herb*____ in my country. The plant
                          1

has small dark green _____ . It has a fresh smell. We
                          2

used to grow mint in our garden when I was a _____ .
                                                    3

We dried the leaves and made _____ from them. It helps
                                  4

with _____ and upset stomachs. We usually drank mint tea after every
         5

_____ . Today, I make iced mint tea in the summer.
     6

B Answer the questions about the paragraph in Exercise A.

1. What is a popular herb? ____*Mint.*____

2. What does the plant look like? _____

3. Where did the writer grow mint? _____

4. What did the writer make from the leaves? _____

5. What illnesses is mint tea good for? _____

6. When did the writer's family drink it? _____

7. What does the writer like to make today? _____

C Use the information in the chart to complete the paragraph about lavender.

Name of plant	Appearance	Use dried flowers to . . .
Lavender	Silver-green leaves and tiny purple flowers Beautiful smell	Make tea (treats headaches) Make bath oil (very relaxing) Keep clothes fresh (smell keeps moths away)

_____ is a popular plant. It has _____ and

_____ . It also has a _____ . You can use the

dried flowers to _____ . It helps with _____ . You can also

_____ . It is _____ . Another use is to _____ .

The smell _____ .

Name: _____

Lesson E *Writing*

A Complete the paragraph.

after every meal	popular herb
indigestion and upset stomachs	small dark green leaves
made tea	when I was a child

Mint is a _____*popular herb*_____ in my country.
                        1

The plant has _____ . It has a fresh smell.
                        2

We used to grow mint in our garden _____ .
                                                    3

We dried the leaves and _____ from them. It
                                    4

helps with _____ . We usually drank mint tea
                        5

_____ . Today, I make iced mint tea in the summer.
            6

B Read the paragraph in Exercise A again. Number the questions in the correct order. Then write the answers.

_____ What did the writer make from the leaves? _____

_____ What does the plant look like? _____

_____ What illnesses is mint tea good for? _____

_1_ What is a popular herb? _____*Mint.*_____

_____ What does the writer like to make today? _____

_____ When did the writer's family drink it? _____

_____ Where did the writer grow mint? _____

C Use the information in the chart to write a paragraph about lavender. Add any other information you know about this plant. Use the back of this paper.

Name of plant	Appearance	Use dried flowers to . . .
Lavender	Silver-green leaves and tiny purple flowers Beautiful smell	Make tea (treats headaches) Make bath oil (very relaxing) Keep clothes fresh (smell keeps moths away)

Lesson F Another view

A Match each group of words with a word in the box.

complaint	herbal supplement	illness	injury	medication

1. _complaint_

   back pain   a headache   a sore throat

2. _____

   aspirin   penicillin   ibuprofen

3. _____

   garlic pills   echinacea   ginger

4. _____

   a broken leg   a sprained ankle   a broken arm

5. _____

   flu   a cold   asthma

B Complete the crossword puzzle. Use the correct form of the verbs in the box.

eat	gain	give	go	lose	start

Across

1. My blood pressure has _____ down.
4. I've _____ to exercise every week.
5. I haven't _____ any weight lately.

Down

1. I've _____ up ice cream.
2. I've _____ weight. I feel healthy!
3. I haven't _____ any French fries this month.

C Write two questions to ask your teacher. Use *use to*.

   Example: _Did you use to ride a bike to school?_

   1. _____

   2. _____

Name: _____

Lesson F *Another view*

A Circle the correct answers.

1. An example of a complaint is ____ .
   a. asthma   (c.) back pain
   b. aspirin   d. vitamins

2. An example of medication is ____ .
   a. garlic pills   c. mint tea
   b. aspirin   d. allergies

3. An example of an herbal supplement is ____ .
   a. medicine   c. a stomachache
   b. allergies   d. garlic pills

4. An example of an injury is ____ .
   a. surgery   c. a headache
   b. a cold   d. a broken leg

5. An example of an illness is ____ .
   a. aspirin   c. a sore throat
   b. flu   d. a headache

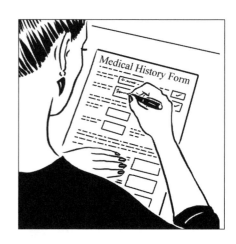

B Complete the crossword puzzle.

			¹g	o	n	e
²l					
	³e				
⁴s						
⁵g					

Across
1. My blood pressure has ____ down.
4. I've ____ to exercise every week.
5. I haven't ____ any weight lately.

Down
1. I've ____ up ice cream.
2. I've ____ weight. I feel healthy!
3. I haven't ____ any French fries this month.

C Write three questions to ask your teacher. Use *use to*.

Example: *Did you use to ride a bike to school?*

1. _____

2. _____

3. _____

A Write two more examples for each category. Use the words in the box.

a broken arm	a headache	a sprained ankle	echinacea	ibuprofen
a cold	a sore throat	asthma	ginger	penicillin

1. A complaint:

   a. back pain   b. *a headache*   c. _____

2. A medication:

   a. aspirin   b. _____   c. _____

3. An herbal supplement:

   a. garlic pills   b. _____   c. _____

4. An injury:

   a. a broken leg   b. _____   c. _____

5. An illness:

   a. flu   b. _____   c. _____

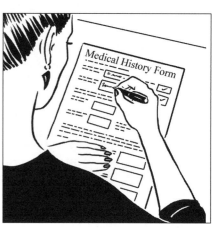

B Complete the crossword puzzle.

Across

1. My blood pressure has _____ down.
4. I've _____ to exercise every week.
5. I haven't _____ any weight lately.

Down

1. I've _____ up ice cream.
2. I've _____ weight. I feel healthy!
3. I haven't _____ any French fries this month.

C Write four questions to ask the teacher. Use *use to*.

Example: *Did you use to ride a bike to school?*

1. _____

2. _____

3. _____

4. _____

Lesson A Get ready

☑ ■ ■

A Match the words with the definitions.

1. exhibit __c__   a. a performance of music or dance

2. concert ____   b. choices

3. tour ____   c. a presentation

4. afford ____   d. a short trip or guided walk

5. admission ____   e. to have enough money to buy something

6. options ____   f. the price you pay to enter an event or place

B Complete the sentences.

1. Leon loves paintings. He's going to the (art exhibit)/ **dance concert**.

2. Jun's children love stories. They're going to the **community barbecue** /

   storytelling at the library.

3. Sam loves flowers. He's going **on the garden tour** / **to the art exhibit**.

4. Khalid loves classical music. He's going to the **storytelling at the library** / **piano concert**.

5. Shamira loves dancing. She's going to the **art exhibit** / **dance concert**.

6. Rosita loves cooking. She's going to the **community barbecue** / **piano concert**.

C Choose an event from Exercise B. Complete the conversation.

You Let's go to the _____ at the

_____ .

Friend Good idea! What time does it _____ ?

You It starts at _____ .

Friend How much is the admission?

You It costs _____ .

Friend OK. I'll meet you _____ .

Lesson A *Get ready*

A Write the words for the definitions.

1. e <u>x</u> <u>h</u> <u>i</u> <u>b</u> <u>i</u> <u>t</u> : a presentation

2. c __ __ __ __ __ __ : a performance of music or dance

3. t __ __ __ : a short trip or guided walk

4. a __ __ __ __ __ : to have enough money to buy something

5. a __ __ __ __ __ __ __ __ : the price you pay to enter an event or place

6. o __ __ __ __ __ __ : choices

B Complete the sentences with the phrases in the box.

art exhibit	dance concert	piano concert
community barbecue	garden tour	storytelling at the library

1. Leon loves paintings. He's going to the _____ *art exhibit* _____ .

2. Jun's children love stories. They're going to the _____ .

3. Sam loves flowers. He's going on the _____ .

4. Khalid loves classical music. He's going to the _____ .

5. Shamira loves dancing. She's going to the _____ .

6. Rosita likes cooking. She's going to the _____ .

C Choose an event from Exercise B. Complete the conversation.

You Let's go to the _____ at the _____ .

Friend Good idea! What time does it _____ ?

You It starts at _____ .

Friend How much is the admission?

You It costs _____ .

Friend OK. I'll meet you _____ .

You If the weather is nice, we can _____ after the _____ .

Lesson A *Get ready*   ■ ■ ☑

A Write the words for the definitions.

1. e*xhibit*_____: a presentation

2. c_____: a performance of music or dance

3. t_____: a short trip or guided walk

4. a_____: to have enough money to buy something

5. a_____: the price you pay to enter an event or place

6. o_____: choices

B Complete the sentences with an event.

1. Leon loves paintings. He's going to the art _____*exhibit*_____ .

2. Jun's children love stories. They're going to the _____ at the library.

3. Sam loves flowers. He's going on the garden _____ .

4. Khalid loves classical music. He's going to the piano _____ .

5. Shamira loves dancing. She's going to the dance _____ .

6. Rosita likes cooking. She's going to the community _____ .

C Choose an event from Exercise B. Complete the conversation.

You Let's go to the _____ at the _____ .

Friend Good idea! What time does it _____ ?

You It starts at _____ .

Friend How much is the admission?

You It costs _____ .

Friend OK. I'll meet you _____ .

You If the weather is nice, we can _____ after the _____ .

Friend Or we can _____ .

You See you later, then.

Lesson B *Verbs + infinitives*

A Complete the questions. Use a verb and the infinitive.

1. **A** What time did you __*agree to meet*__ Cindy?

   B I agreed to meet her at 5:00 p.m.

2. **A** How much can you _____ on the tickets?

   B I can afford to spend about $20.

3. **A** Where do you _____ on weekends?

   B We like to go to the park.

4. **A** When do you _____ your vacation?

   B I plan to take my vacation next week.

5. **A** What do you _____ at the mall?

   B I need to buy some new boots.

6. **A** What have you _____ to the party?

   B I've decided to wear my red dress.

B Read Wanda's calendar. Complete the paragraph. Use infinitives.

buy	get up	go	have	meet	pay	play	visit

What does Wanda plan to do on Saturday?

First, she plans __*to get up*__ early because she
             1

wants _____ tennis with Suzy. Then she
          2

needs _____ some food. She has agreed
          3

_____ lunch with Charlie at 12:30 p.m. After
        4

lunch, they would like _____ the art
                    5

museum. In the evening, she expects _____
                                   6

Dina for dinner at 6:00 p.m. She has promised _____ with Dina to a concert at 8:00 p.m.
                                          7

But the ticket is a little expensive, and she is worried that she can't afford _____ for it.
                                                                      8

Saturday

6:00 a.m. get up early
6:30 a.m. play tennis with Suzy
9:00 a.m. buy food – urgent!
12:30 p.m. have lunch with Charlie
2:00 p.m. visit the art museum
6:00 p.m. meet Dina for dinner
8:00 p.m. go to concert with Dina

C What do you plan to do this weekend? Write a sentence.

I plan _____ .

Name: _____

Lesson **B** *Verbs + infinitives*

A Complete the questions and answers. Use the verbs in parentheses with the verbs in the box.

buy	go	meet	spend	take	wear

1. (agree) **A** What time did you __*agree to meet*__ Cindy?

   B I __*agreed to meet*__ her at 5:00 p.m.

2. (afford) **A** How much can you _____ on the tickets?

   B I can _____ about $20.

3. (like) **A** Where do you _____ on weekends?

   B We _____ to the park.

4. (plan) **A** When do you _____ your vacation?

   B I _____ my vacation next week.

5. (need) **A** What do you _____ at the mall?

   B I _____ some new boots.

6. (decide) **A** What have you _____ to the party?

   B I've _____ my red dress.

B Read Wanda's calendar. Complete the paragraph. Use infinitives.

What does Wanda plan to do on Saturday?

First, she plans __*to get up*__ early because she
1

wants _____ tennis with Suzy. Then she
2

needs _____ some food. She has agreed
3

_____ lunch with Charlie at 12:30 p.m. After
4

lunch, they would like _____ the art
5

museum. In the evening, she expects _____
6

Saturday
6:00 a.m. get up early
6:30 a.m. play tennis with Suzy
9:00 a.m. buy food – urgent!
12:30 p.m. have lunch with Charlie
2:00 p.m. visit the art museum
6:00 p.m. meet Dina for dinner
8:00 p.m. go to concert with Dina

Dina for dinner at 6:00 p.m. She has promised _____ with Dina to a concert at 8:00 p.m.
7

But the ticket is a little expensive, and she is worried that she can't afford _____ for it.
8

C What do you plan to do this weekend? Write three sentences. Use *plan*, *want*, and *would like*. Use the back of this paper.

Lesson **B** *Verbs + infinitives*

A Complete the questions and answers. Use one verb from each box.

afford	decide	need
agree	like	plan

buy	meet	take
go	spend	wear

1. **A** What time did you _agree to meet_ Cindy?

   B I _agreed to meet_ her at 5:00 p.m.

2. **A** How much can you _____ on the tickets?

   B I can _____ about $20.

3. **A** Where do you _____ on weekends?

   B We _____ to the park.

4. **A** When do you _____ your vacation?

   B I _____ my vacation next week.

5. **A** What do you _____ at the mall?

   B I _____ some new boots.

6. **A** What have you _____ to the party?

   B I've _____ my red dress.

B Read Wanda's calendar. Complete the paragraph. Use the verbs in the box and infinitives.

afford	expect	need	promise
agree	like	plan	want

Saturday

| 6:00 a.m. get up early |
| 6:30 a.m. play tennis with Suzy |
| 9:00 a.m. buy food – urgent! |
| 12:30 p.m. have lunch with Charlie |
| 2:00 p.m. visit the art museum |
| 6:00 p.m. meet Dina for dinner |
| 8:00 p.m. go to concert with Dina |

What does Wanda plan to do on Saturday?

First, she p_lans_ _to get up_ early because she
$_1$

w_____ tennis with Suzy. Then she
$_2$

n_____ some food. She has
$_3$

a_____ lunch with Charlie at 12:30 p.m.
$_4$

After lunch, they would l_____ the art museum. In the evening, she
$_5$

e_____ Dina for dinner at 6:00 p.m. She has p_____ with Dina to
$_6$ $_7$

a concert at 8:00 p.m. But the ticket is a little expensive, and she is worried that she can't

a_____ for it.
$_8$

C What do you plan to do this weekend? Write a paragraph. Use the back of this paper.

Name:

A Look at the picture. Circle the correct verb.

1. The birthday party **has** / **hasn't** started yet.

2. Tom **has** / **hasn't** set up the table already.

3. We **have** / **haven't** put up the decorations already.

4. I **has** / **have** made the food already.

5. You **have** / **haven't** brought out the food yet.

6. Our friends **have** / **haven't** arrived yet.

B Write questions and answers about the events.

What's Around Town				
Afternoon movies Wednesday 3 p.m., 5 p.m. $5	**Salsa concert** Friday night 8 til late	**Book fair** 200 vendors Saturdays 11 a.m.–4 p.m.	**English café** Tea and coffee served every day 8 a.m.–8 p.m.	**Yoga classes** Beginners welcome Start Nov. 5

1. (start) **A** It's 2:00 p.m. on Wednesday. _Has_ the movie _started_ yet?

   B No, it hasn't.

2. (end) **A** It's 3:30 p.m. on Wednesday. _____ the movie _____ yet?

   B No, it hasn't.

3. (begin) **A** It's 9:00 p.m. on Friday. _____ the concert _____ already?

   B Yes, it has.

4. (close) **A** It's 5:00 p.m. on Saturday. _____ the book vendors _____ already?

   B Yes, they have.

5. (open) **A** It's 7:00 a.m. on Wednesday. _____ the English café _____ yet?

   B No, it hasn't.

6. (start) **A** It's November 6. _____ the yoga classes _____ yet?

   B Yes, they have.

Name: _____

Lesson **C** *Present perfect*

A Look at the picture. Complete the sentences. Use the present perfect.

1. The birthday party ___*hasn't started*___ yet.
   (start)

2. Tom _____ the table already.
   (set up)

3. We _____ the decorations already.
   (put up)

4. I _____ the food already.
   (make)

5. You _____ the food yet.
   (bring out)

6. Our friends _____ yet.
   (arrive)

B Write questions and answers about the events.

What's Around Town				
Afternoon movies Wednesday 3 p.m., 5 p.m. $5	**Salsa concert** Friday night 8 til late	**Book fair** 200 vendors Saturdays 11 a.m.–4 p.m.	**English café** Tea and coffee served every day 8 a.m.–8 p.m.	**Yoga classes** Beginners welcome Start Nov. 5

1. (start) **A** It's 2:00 p.m. on Wednesday. ___*Has*___ the movie ___*started*___ yet?

   B No, ___*it hasn't*___ .

2. (end) **A** It's 3:30 p.m. on Wednesday. _____ the movie _____ yet?

   B No, _____ .

3. (begin) **A** It's 9:00 p.m. on Friday. _____ the concert _____ already?

   B Yes, _____ .

4. (close) **A** It's 5:00 p.m. on Saturday. _____ the book vendors _____ already?

   B Yes, _____ .

5. (open) **A** It's 7:00 a.m. on Wednesday. _____ the English café _____ yet?

   B No, _____ .

6. (start) **A** It's November 6th. _____ the yoga classes _____ yet?

   B Yes, _____ .

Name: _____

Lesson C *Present perfect*

A Complete the sentences. Use the present perfect.

arrive	bring out	make	put up	set up	start

1. The birthday party ___*hasn't started*___ yet.
2. Tom _____ the table already.
3. We _____ the decorations already.
4. I _____ the food already.
5. You _____ the food yet.
6. Our friends _____ yet.

B Write questions and answers about the events.

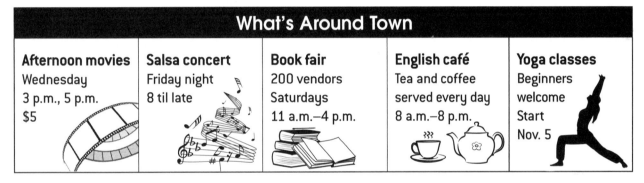

What's Around Town				
Afternoon movies Wednesday 3 p.m., 5 p.m. $5	**Salsa concert** Friday night 8 til late	**Book fair** 200 vendors Saturdays 11 a.m.–4 p.m.	**English café** Tea and coffee served every day 8 a.m.–8 p.m.	**Yoga classes** Beginners welcome Start Nov. 5

1. **A** It's 2:00 p.m. on Wednesday. ___*Has the movie started*___ yet?
   (start / movie)
   B ___*No, it hasn't.*___

2. **A** It's 3:30 p.m. on Wednesday. _____ yet?
   (end / movie)
   B _____

3. **A** It's 9:00 p.m. on Friday. _____ already?
   (begin / concert)
   B _____

4. **A** It's 5:00 p.m. on Saturday. _____ already?
   (close / book vendors)
   B _____

5. **A** It's 7:00 a.m. on Wednesday. _____ yet?
   (open / café)
   B _____

6. **A** It's November 6. _____ yet?
   (start / yoga classes)
   B _____

Lesson D Reading

A Read the article. Circle the correct answers.

Paris Fashion Show

Carlos Emanuel's winter fashion collection at the Paris Plaza Hotel last Saturday was a sensational explosion of brilliant pink, red, and orange.

Introducing the show was a newcomer to the fashion scene, Maria La Paz. Gray, cream, and brown were her main color themes. The designs and the colors were plain and unremarkable. The music was loud and irritating.

In the second part of the show, Carlos Emanuel's creative collection was an amazing contrast. There were many versatile designs for day or evening, for office or leisure. The lights and music for his show were also superb. Is bright pink a little excessive for the office? No way! Everyone in the audience loved it. So look for exciting colors – red, pink, and orange – in the stores this winter.

---

1. The reviewer liked **the first part** / (**the second part**) of the fashion show.

2. Maria La Paz chose colors that were **bright** / **unremarkable**.

3. The music for Maria La Paz's fashions was **irritating** / **superb**.

4. Carlos Emanuel chose colors that were **exciting** / **plain**.

5. The reviewer thought that Emanuel's show was **sensational** / **OK**.

B Circle the correct meanings according to the article. Put a check (✓) next to the positive words and an X next to the negative words.

1. _✓_ sensational   a. terrible   (b. fantastic)

2. ____ unremarkable   a. exciting   b. boring

3. ____ irritating   a. unpleasant   b. quiet

4. ____ amazing   a. great   b. pleasant

5. ____ superb   a. nice   b. excellent

6. ____ excessive   a. too much   b. too little

C Write two sentences about a type of music or a singer that you like or dislike. Use two adjectives from this lesson.

1. _____

2. _____

     © Cambridge University Press 2008 **Photocopiable**

Lesson D Reading

A Read the article. Circle the correct answers.

Paris Fashion Show

Carlos Emanuel's winter fashion collection at the Paris Plaza Hotel last Saturday was a sensational explosion of brilliant pink, red, and orange.

Introducing the show was a newcomer to the fashion scene, Maria La Paz. Gray, cream, and brown were her main color themes. The designs and the colors were plain and unremarkable. The music was loud and irritating.

In the second part of the show, Carlos Emanuel's creative collection was an amazing contrast. There were many versatile designs for day or evening, for office or leisure. The lights and music for his show were also superb. Is bright pink a little excessive for the office? No way! Everyone in the audience loved it. So look for exciting colors – red, pink, and orange – in the stores this winter.

---

1. The reviewer liked **the first part** / (**the second part**) / **both parts** of the fashion show.

2. Maria La Paz chose colors that were **bright** / **irritating** / **unremarkable**.

3. The music for Maria La Paz's fashions was **interesting** / **irritating** / **superb**.

4. Carlos Emanuel chose colors that were **exciting** / **excessive** / **plain**.

5. The reviewer thought that Emanuel's show was **sensational** / **good** / **OK**.

B Circle the correct meanings according to the article. Put a check (✓) next to the positive words and an X next to the negative words.

1. ✓ sensational   a. terrible   (b. fantastic)   c. interesting

2. ____ unremarkable   a. exciting   b. boring   c. nice

3. ____ irritating   a. unpleasant   b. quiet   c. excellent

4. ____ amazing   a. great   b. pleasant   c. unremarkable

5. ____ superb   a. nice   b. terrible   c. excellent

6. ____ excessive   a. too much   b. too little   c. too creative

C Write three sentences about a type of music or a singer that you like or dislike. Use three adjectives from this lesson. Use the back of this paper.

Name: _____

Lesson **D** *Reading*

A Read the article. Replace one word in each sentence so that it is correct. Use the words in the box.

Paris Fashion Show

Carlos Emanuel's winter fashion collection at the Paris Plaza Hotel last Saturday was a sensational explosion of brilliant pink, red, and orange.

Introducing the show was a newcomer to the fashion scene, Maria La Paz. Gray, cream, and brown were her main color themes. The designs and the colors were plain and unremarkable. The music was loud and irritating.

In the second part of the show, Carlos Emanuel's creative collection was an amazing contrast. There were many versatile designs for day or evening, for office or leisure. The lights and music for his show were also superb. Is bright pink a little excessive for the office? No way! Everyone in the audience loved it. So look for exciting colors – red, pink, and orange – in the stores this winter.

---

exciting	irritating	second	sensational	unremarkable

             second
1. The reviewer liked the ~~first~~ part of the fashion show.

2. Maria La Paz chose colors that were bright.

3. The music for Maria La Paz's fashions was pleasant.

4. Carlos Emanuel chose colors that were boring.

5. The reviewer thought that Emanuel's show was OK.

B Match the words with their meanings in this article. Put a check (✓) next to the positive words and an X next to the negative words.

1. ___✓___ sensational __c__   a. boring

2. _____ unremarkable _____   b. too much

3. _____ irritating _____   c. fantastic

4. _____ amazing _____   d. excellent

5. _____ superb _____   e. unpleasant

6. _____ excessive _____   f. great

C Write four sentences about a type of music or a singer that you like or dislike. Use four adjectives from this lesson. Use the back of this paper.

A Are these comments positive or negative? Write the comments in the chart.

Baseball Game
The Tigers were incredible.
The weather was cold and rainy.
The hot dogs were awful.
The game was really exciting.

Classic Rockers Concert
The Classic Rockers were awesome.
We had excellent seats near the stage.
The sound level was too loud.
I got a headache.

Name of event	Positive information	Negative information
Baseball Game Lions v. Tigers Saturday 2:00 p.m.	*The Tigers were incredible.*	
Rock Concert Classic Rockers Band Replay Music Club Saturday 8:00 p.m.		

B Complete the notes. Use information from Exercise A.

Hi Pete,

The baseball game on Saturday afternoon was fabulous. The Tigers were ___incredible___ .

The game was _____ . We ate hot dogs and popcorn. The hot dogs

were _____ . One problem: the weather. It was _____ and we

didn't have umbrellas. Come with us next time!

Andy

Hi Andy,

The rock concert on Saturday night was fantastic. The Classic Rockers were _____ .

They are superb musicians. We could see everything. We had _____

near the stage. One problem: the sound level. It was _____ and I

_____ . Come with us next time!

Pete

A Are these comments positive or negative? Which event do they go with?
Write the comments in the chart.

The Tigers were incredible.	We had excellent seats near the stage.
The weather was cold and rainy.	The sound level was too loud.
The Classic Rockers were awesome.	The hot dogs were awful.
The game was really exciting.	I got a headache.

Name of event	Positive information	Negative information
Baseball Game Lions v. Tigers Saturday 2:00 p.m.	*The Tigers were incredible.*	
Rock Concert Classic Rockers Band Replay Music Club Saturday 8:00 p.m.		

B Complete the notes. Use information from Exercise A.

Hi Pete,

The baseball game on Saturday afternoon was fabulous. *The Tigers were incredible* .

The game _____ . We ate hot dogs and popcorn. _____

_____ One problem: the weather. It was _____

_____ and we didn't have umbrellas. Come with us next time!

Andy

Hi Andy,

The _____ on Saturday night was fantastic. _____

_____ They are superb musicians. We could see everything.

_____ One problem: the sound level.

It was _____ and I _____ . Come with us

next time!

Pete

Name: _____

Lesson **E** *Writing*

A Are these comments positive or negative? Which event do they go with? Write the comments in the chart.

The Tigers were incredible.	The game was really exciting.
They are superb musicians.	The sound level was too loud.
I got a headache.	The Classic Rockers were awesome.
We didn't have umbrellas.	We had excellent seats near the stage.
The hot dogs were awful.	The weather was cold and rainy.

Name of event	Positive information	Negative information
Baseball Game Lions v. Tigers Saturday 2:00 p.m.	*The Tigers were incredible.*	
Rock Concert Classic Rockers Band Replay Music Club Saturday 8:00 p.m.		

B Complete the notes. Use information from Exercise A.

Hi Pete,

The baseball game on Saturday afternoon was fabulous. *The Tigers were incredible.*

_____ We ate hot dogs and popcorn. _____

_____ One problem: the weather. It _____

and we _____ . Come with us next time!

Andy

Hi Andy,

The rock concert on Saturday night was fantastic. _____

_____ We could see everything. _____

_____ One problem: the sound level. It _____

_____ and I _____ . Come with us next time!

Pete

Lesson F *Another view*

Name: _____

A Read the announcements. Write the best event for each person.

Home Improvement Workshop Learn to fix pipes and broken lights. Improve your home and save money. 9:00 a.m. – 4:00 p.m. Saturday $20	**French Film Festival** Saturday and Sunday 1:30 p.m., 4:00 p.m., 5:30 p.m., 8:00 p.m. Tickets $5 All-day pass $15
Herbal Garden Tour Garden tour and herbal tea tasting. Herbal plant sale Sunday 2:00 p.m. Free	**Animal Shelter Adoption Day** Find out how to take care of your pet. Find a pet for your family. Sunday 10:00 a.m. – 4:00 p.m. $5 donation

1. Sasha loves to make herbal tea.   *Herbal Garden Tour*

2. David likes to take care of animals.   _____

3. Rani needs to fix her kitchen sink.   _____

4. Beth used to study French.   _____

B Complete the crossword puzzle with words from this unit.

Down

1. The movie had a lot of action. It was very ____ .
2. My favorite band is going to give a ____ on Saturday. Let's get tickets.
3. The trip was fantastic. It was ____ .
4. The game was very bad. It was ____ .
5. The musicians were excellent. They were ____ .

Across

4. The museum charges $15 for ____ .

© Cambridge University Press 2008 **Photocopiable**

Name: _____

Lesson **F** *Another view*

A Read the announcements. Complete the sentences with words from the box. Write the best event for each person.

Home Improvement Workshop Learn to fix pipes and broken lights. Improve your home and save money. 9:00 a.m. – 4:00 p.m. Saturday $20	**French Film Festival** Saturday and Sunday 1:30 p.m., 4:00 p.m., 5:30 p.m., 8:00 p.m. Tickets $5 All-day pass $15
Herbal Garden Tour Garden tour and herbal tea tasting. Herbal plant sale Sunday 2:00 p.m. Free	**Animal Shelter Adoption Day** Find out how to take care of your pet. Find a pet for your family. Sunday 10:00 a.m. – 4:00 p.m. $5 donation

her kitchen sink	herbal tea	French	animals

1. Sasha loves to make *herbal tea* .   *Herbal Garden Tour*

2. David likes to take care of _____ .   _____

3. Rani needs to fix _____ .   _____

4. Beth used to study _____ .   _____

B Complete the crossword puzzle with words from this unit.

Down

1. The movie had a lot of action. It was very ____ .
2. My favorite band is going to give a ____ on Saturday. Let's get tickets.
3. The trip was fantastic. It was ____ .
4. The game was very bad. It was ____ .
5. The musicians were excellent. They were ____ .

Across

4. The museum charges $15 for ____ .

Lesson F *Another view*

A Read the announcements. Complete the sentences. Use words from both boxes.

Home Improvement Workshop Learn to fix pipes and broken lights. Improve your home and save money. 9:00 a.m. – 4:00 p.m. Saturday $20	**French Film Festival** Saturday and Sunday 1:30 p.m., 4:00 p.m., 5:30 p.m., 8:00 p.m. Tickets $5 All-day pass $15
Herbal Garden Tour Garden tour and herbal tea tasting. Herbal plant sale Sunday 2:00 p.m. Free	**Animal Shelter Adoption Day** Find out how to take care of your pet. Find a pet for your family. Sunday 10:00 a.m. – 4:00 p.m. $5 donation

| fix   make   study   take care of | | animals   French   herbal tea   her kitchen sink |

1. Sasha loves to _make herbal tea_____ .

   She should take the Herbal Garden Tour. Admission is _____free._____ .

2. David likes to _____ .

   He should go to the Animal Shelter Adoption Day. Admission is _____ .

3. Rani needs to _____ .

   She should go to the Home Improvement Workshop. Admission is _____ .

4. Beth used to _____ .

   She should go to the French Film Festival. Admission is _____ .

B Complete the crossword puzzle with words from this unit. What is the mystery word?

Down
1. The movie had a lot of action. It was very _____ .
2. My favorite band is going to give a _____ on Saturday.
   Let's get tickets.
3. The trip was fantastic. It was _____ .
4. The game was very bad. It was _____ .
5. The musicians were excellent. They were _____ .

Across
4. ?

(Crossword grid with vertical word: e x c i t i n g)

Lesson A *Get ready*

A Match the words with their definitions.

1. deadline __d__   a. anxious or restless

2. impatient ____   b. put things in order of importance

3. procrastinating ____   c. tasks around the house

4. chores ____   d. date when something is due

5. prioritize ____   e. delaying

B Complete the paragraph. Use the words from Exercise A.

Right now I have many things to do. It is important to _____*prioritize*_____ . I should

make a to-do list. First, I have a lot of _____ to do around the house.

Secondly, my project is due tomorrow. The _____ is ten o'clock. When I hand

in an assignment, I usually feel _____ because I want to know the result

immediately. I also have to practice the piano because I have a concert next month. I need to

manage my time better. Unfortunately, I'm good at _____ .

C Look at the to-do list. Circle the correct answers.

1. How many chores are on Veronica's list?
   a. five chores
   b. six chores

2. What will she do first?
   a. do grocery shopping
   b. clean the house

3. When is the deadline for her project?
   a. Sunday
   b. Monday

4. What will she do if she has time?
   a. practice the guitar
   b. finish her Internet project

> Veronica's to-do list
>
> Clean the house
>
> Do grocery shopping
>
> Cook dinner
>
> Finish Internet project –
> due Monday
>
> Practice the guitar, if time

D Answer the questions about yourself.

1. When do you feel impatient?

_____

2. What kind of chores do you dislike the most?

_____

Lesson A *Get ready*

A Write the words for the definitions.

1. d <u>e a d l i n e</u> : date when something is due

2. i __ __ __ __ __ __ __ __ __ : anxious or restless

3. p __ __ __ __ __ __ __ __ __ __ __ __ __ : delaying

4. c __ __ __ __ __ : tasks around the house

5. p __ __ __ __ __ __ __ __ __ : put in order of importance

B Complete the paragraph. Use the words from Exercise A and the words in the box.

due	list	manage	practice

Right now, I have many things to do. It is important to _____*prioritize*_____ . I

should make a to-do _____ . First, I have a lot of _____

to do around the house. Secondly, my project is _____ tomorrow. The

_____ is ten o'clock. When I hand in an assignment, I usually feel

_____ because I want to know the result immediately. I also have

to _____ the piano because I have a concert next month. I need to

_____ my time better. Unfortunately, I'm good at _____ .

C Look at the to-do list. Answer the questions.

1. How many chores are on Veronica's list?
   There are five chores on Veronica's list.

2. What will she do first?
   _____

3. When is the deadline for her project?
   _____

4. What will she do if she has time?
   _____

> Veronica's to-do list
>
> Clean the house
> Do grocery shopping
> Cook dinner
> Finish Internet project –
> due Monday
> Practice the guitar, if time

D Answer the questions about yourself. Use the back of this paper.

1. When do you feel impatient?

2. What kind of chores do you dislike the most?

3. What do you do when you have a deadline?

Lesson A Get ready ■.■■ ☑

A Write the words for the definitions.

1. d_____ : date when something is due

2. i_____ : anxious or restless

3. p_____ : delaying

4. c_____ : tasks around the house

5. p_____ : put in order of importance

B Complete the paragraph. Use the words from Exercise A and the words in the box.

assignment	concert	due	list	manage	practice

Right now, I have many things to do. It is important to _____*prioritize*_____ . I

should make a to-do _____ . First, I have a lot of _____

to do around the house. Secondly, my project is _____ tomorrow. The

_____ is ten o'clock. When I hand in an _____ , I usually

feel _____ because I want to know the result immediately. I also have to

_____ the piano because I have a _____ next month. I need

to _____ my time better. Unfortunately, I'm good at _____ .

C Look at the to-do list. Write questions.

1. *How many chores are on Veronica's list?*

   There are five chores on Veronica's list.

2. _____

   She will clean the house first.

3. _____

   The deadline for her project is Monday.

4. _____

   She will practice the guitar if she has time.

> Veronica's to-do list
>
> Clean the house
>
> Do grocery shopping
>
> Cook dinner
>
> Finish Internet project – due Monday
>
> Practice the guitar, if time

D Answer the questions about yourself. Use the back of this paper.

1. When do you feel impatient?

2. What kind of chores do you dislike the most?

3. What do you do when you have a deadline?

4. When do you need to prioritize your tasks?

Lesson B Dependent clauses

A Make sentences with *when*.

1. Ernesto / have many things to do / make a to-do list

   When Ernesto has many things to do, he makes a to-do list.

2. Felicia / have to do some research / go on the Internet

   _____

3. I / need to finish my work on time / set a deadline

   _____

4. we / have a test the next day / go to bed early

   _____

5. they / want to concentrate / turn off the TV

   _____

B Complete the questions. Use information from Exercise A.

1. What does Ernesto do when *he has many things to do* _____ ?

   He makes a to-do list.

2. What does Felicia do when _____ ?

   She goes on the Internet.

3. What do you do when _____ ?

   I set a deadline.

4. What do you do when _____ ?

   We go to bed early.

5. What do they do when _____ ?

   They turn off the TV.

C What tip do you have for managing your time? Write your idea. Use *when*.

   _____

Lesson B *Dependent clauses*

A Make sentences with *when*. Use the phrases in the box.

goes on the Internet	makes a to-do list	turn off the TV
go to bed early	set a deadline	

1. Ernesto / have many things to do

   When Ernesto has many things to do, he makes a to-do list.

2. Felicia / have to do some research

   _____

3. I / need to finish my work on time

   _____

4. we / have a test the next day

   _____

5. they / want to concentrate

   _____

B Write questions for these answers. Use information from Exercise A.

1. *What does Ernesto do when he has many things to do?*

   He makes a to-do list.

2. _____

   She goes on the Internet.

3. _____

   I set a deadline.

4. _____

   We go to bed early.

5. _____

   They turn off the TV.

C What tips do you have for managing your time? Write two ideas. Use *when*.

1. _____

2. _____

Lesson B *Dependent clauses*

A Make sentences with *when*. Use the correct form of the phrases in the box.

go on the Internet	make a to-do list	turn off the TV
go to bed early	set a deadline	

1. Ernesto / have many things to do

   When Ernesto has many things to do, he makes a to-do list.

2. Felicia / have to do some research

   _____

3. I / need to finish my work on time

   _____

4. we / have a test the next day

   _____

5. they / want to concentrate

   _____

B Write questions and answers. Use information from Exercise A.

1. *What does Ernesto do when he has many things to do?*

   He _____ . (to-do list)

2. _____

   She _____ . (Internet)

3. _____

   I _____ . (deadline)

4. _____

   We _____ . (bed early)

5. _____

   They _____ . (TV)

C What tips do you have for managing your time? Write three ideas. Use *when*.

1. _____

2. _____

3. _____

Lesson C *Dependent clauses*

A Look at the pictures of Sun-mi. Write sentences with *before* or *after*.

buy vegetables   put on her uniform   make the dessert   take a break

1. buys vegetables / goes to work

    After *Sun-mi buys vegetables, she goes to work* _____ .

2. puts on her uniform / starts work

    _____ before _____ .

3. cooks the vegetables / makes the dessert

    Before _____ .

4. takes a break / prepares the meal

    _____ after _____ .

B Write sentences. Use *before* or *after*.

1. Sandy studies in the library. Then she goes to school.

    Sandy studies in the library before *she goes to school* _____ .

2. Sofia puts on her makeup. Then she goes to work.

    After _____ .

3. Tam reads the newspaper. Then he has breakfast.

    Before _____ .

4. Shin cooks dinner. Then she watches TV.

    After _____ .

C Write two sentences about things you do every day. Use *before* or *after*.

1. _____

2. _____

Name: _____

Lesson C *Dependent clauses*

A Look at the pictures of Sun-mi. Make sentences with *before* or *after*.

buy vegetables   put on her uniform   make the dessert   take a break

1. After / buy vegetables / go to work

   After Sun-mi buys vegetables, she goes to work.

2. put on her uniform / before / start work

   _____

3. Before / cook the vegetables / make the dessert

   _____

4. take a break / after / prepare the meal

   _____

B Write sentences. Use *before* or *after*.

1. Sandy studies in the library. Then she goes to school. (before)

   Sandy studies in the library before she goes to school.

2. Sofia puts on her makeup. Then she goes to work. (After)

   _____

3. Tam reads the newspaper. Then he has breakfast. (Before)

   _____

4. Shin cooks dinner. Then she watches TV. (After)

   _____

C Write three sentences about things you do every day. Use *before* or *after*. Use the back of this paper.

Lesson C Dependent clauses

A Look at the pictures of Sun-mi. Write sentences with *before* or *after*.

buy vegetables   put on her uniform   make the dessert   take a break

1. buy vegetables / go to work (After)

   After Sun-mi buys vegetables, she goes to work.

2. put on her uniform / start work (before)

   _____

3. cook the vegetables / make the dessert (Before)

   _____

4. take a break / prepare the meal (after)

   _____

B Write sentences. Use *before* or *after*.

1. Sandy studies in the library. Then she goes to school. (before)

   Sandy studies in the library before she goes to school.

2. Sofia puts on her makeup. Then she goes to work. (After)

   _____

3. Tam reads the newspaper. Then he has breakfast. (Before)

   _____

4. Shin cooks dinner. Then she watches TV. (After)

   _____

C Write four sentences about things you do every day. Use *before* or *after*.
   Use the back of this paper.

Lesson D *Reading*

A Read the article. Circle the correct answers.

Are You Organized or Disorganized?

Some people are very organized. They write important dates in their calendars. They always remember the birthdays of family and friends. They are never late for appointments. They always have enough time to complete all the tasks on their to-do lists. Organized people feel irresponsible when they lose their watches or their cell phones.

Disorganized people are the complete opposite. They are always late for meetings. They usually forget what time a play or a concert starts and then have to rush at the last minute. They often forget dates – dentist appointments and birthdays, for example – because they never write anything in their calendars. Disorganized people don't feel irresponsible when they lose their watches or cell phones because they are always late anyway.

1. An organized person **writes** / **doesn't write** dates in a calendar.

2. An organized person **is** / **isn't** late for appointments.

3. A disorganized person **is** / **isn't** late for meetings.

4. A disorganized person **feels** / **doesn't feel** irresponsible about losing things.

5. An organized person **has** / **doesn't have** enough time to do everything.

6. A disorganized person **remembers** / **doesn't remember** dates or times.

B Write the words in the correct column.

dishonest	impatient	disorganized	unspoken
uncommon	irregular	irresponsible	impolite

dis-	ir-	im-	un-
dishonest			

C Are you organized or disorganized? Give an example of why.

_____

A Read the article. Complete the sentences.

Are You Organized or Disorganized?

Some people are very organized. They write important dates in their calendars. They always remember the birthdays of family and friends. They are never late for appointments. They always have enough time to complete all the tasks on their to-do lists. Organized people feel irresponsible when they lose their watches or their cell phones.

Disorganized people are the complete opposite. They are always late for meetings. They usually forget what time a play or a concert starts and then have to rush at the last minute. They often forget dates – dentist appointments and birthdays, for example – because they never write anything in their calendars. Disorganized people don't feel irresponsible when they lose their watches or cell phones because they are always late anyway.

| calendar | dates | irresponsible | late | meetings | time |

1. An organized person writes dates in a _____*calendar*_____ .

2. An organized person isn't _____ for appointments.

3. A disorganized person is late for _____ .

4. A disorganized person doesn't feel _____ about losing things.

5. An organized person has enough _____ to do everything.

6. A disorganized person doesn't remember _____ or times.

B Write the opposites of the words in the correct column.

| common | honest | organized | patient | polite | regular | responsible | spoken |

dis-	ir-	im-	un-
dishonest			

C Are you organized or disorganized? Give two examples of why.

1. _____

2. _____

A Read the article. Complete the sentences.

Are You Organized or Disorganized?

Some people are very organized. They write important dates in their calendars. They always remember the birthdays of family and friends. They are never late for appointments. They always have enough time to complete all the tasks on their to-do lists. Organized people feel irresponsible when they lose their watches or their cell phones.

Disorganized people are the complete opposite. They are always late for meetings. They usually forget what time a play or a concert starts and then have to rush at the last minute. They often forget dates – dentist appointments and birthdays, for example – because they never write anything in their calendars. Disorganized people don't feel irresponsible when they lose their watches or cell phones because they are always late anyway.

---

1. *An organized* _____ person writes dates *in a calendar* _____ .

2. _____ person isn't _____ for appointments.

3. _____ person is late for _____ .

4. _____ person doesn't feel _____ about losing things.

5. _____ person has enough _____ to do everything.

6. _____ person doesn't remember _____ or times.

B Write the opposites of the words in the chart. Add a word to each column.

common   honest   organized   patient   polite   regular   responsible   spoken

dis-	ir-	im-	un-
dishonest			

C Are you organized or disorganized? Give three examples of why.

1. _____

2. _____

3. _____

Lesson E *Writing*

A Circle the correct adjective.

1. **Organized /** **Disorganized** people often forget their homework.

2. **Patient / Impatient** people get angry when you are late.

3. **Polite / Impolite** people don't say "thank you."

4. **Organized / Disorganized** people make a to-do list.

5. **Patient / Impatient** people always wait for you.

6. **Polite / Impolite** people always say "hello."

B Complete the paragraph. Use the words in the box.

absent	call	homework	late
borrows	doesn't	irresponsible	successful

Samara is a very ___*irresponsible*___ person. She is always

_____ for work. She never hands in her _____

on time. When she _____ something, she doesn't give it back.

When she is _____ from class, she doesn't _____

the teacher to explain why. After she goes to a job interview, she

_____ write a thank-you note. In summary, Samara isn't very

_____ because she is irresponsible.

C Gerald is the opposite of Samara. Rewrite the paragraph in Exercise B to tell about Gerald.

Gerald is a very ___*responsible*___ person. He is _____

late for work. He _____ hands in his homework on time.

When he borrows something, he _____ it back. When

he is absent from class, he _____ the teacher to explain

why. After he _____ to a job interview, he writes a

_____ note. In summary, Gerald is very successful because he

is _____ .

D Write about a friend who is polite, organized, or patient. Give one example of his or her behavior.

_____

_____

Lesson **E** *Writing*

A Match.

1. Disorganized people _*d*_   a. get angry when you are late.

2. Impatient people ____   b. make a to-do list.

3. Impolite people ____   c. always wait for you.

4. Organized people ____   d. often forget their homework.

5. Patient people ____   e. don't say "thank you."

6. Polite people ____   f. always say "hello."

B Complete the paragraph. Use the words in the box.

doesn't	goes	is	on time	work
explain	irresponsible	isn't	summary	write

Samara is a very ___*irresponsible*___ person. She is always late for

_____ . She never hands in her homework _____ .

When she borrows something, she _____ give it back. When

she _____ absent from class, she doesn't call the teacher to

_____ why. After she _____ to a job interview,

she doesn't _____ a thank-you note. In _____ ,

Samara _____ very successful because she is irresponsible.

C Gerald is the opposite of Samara. Rewrite the paragraph in Exercise B to tell about Gerald.

Gerald _*is a very responsible person*_ . He is _____ .

He always _____ . When _____ ,

_____ . When _____ , he

_____ . After _____ , he

_____ . In summary, Gerald is _____

because _____ .

D Write about a friend who is polite, organized, or patient. Give two examples of his or her behavior.

_____

_____

_____

Lesson E *Writing*

A Complete the sentences. Use one of the adjectives or its opposite.

1. *Disorganized* _____ people often forget their homework.
2. _____ people get angry when you are late.
3. _____ people don't say "thank you."
4. _____ people make a to-do list.
5. _____ people always wait for you.
6. _____ people always say "hello."

| organized |
| patient |
| polite |

B Complete the paragraph.

she doesn't give it back	she doesn't call the teacher
she doesn't write a thank-you note	late for work
is a very irresponsible person	is not very successful

Samara *is a very irresponsible person* . She is always _____ .

She never hands in her homework on time. When she borrows something, _____

_____ . When she is absent from class, _____

to explain why. After she goes to a job interview, _____ .

In summary, Samara _____ because she is irresponsible.

C Gerald is the opposite of Samara. Rewrite the paragraph in Exercise B to
tell about Gerald.

Gerald is a very responsible person. He _____

_____

_____

_____

_____

In summary, Gerald is _____

_____

D Write about a friend who is polite, organized, or patient. Give three
examples of his or her behavior. Use the back of this paper.

Lesson F Another view

A Complete the pie chart. Use the information below.

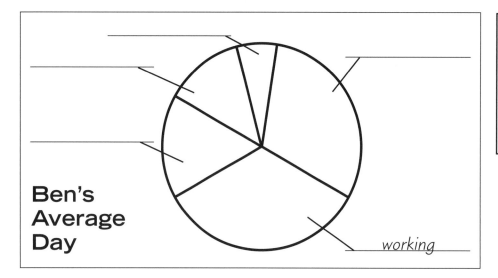

Ben's Average Day

working

Activities
cooking and eating
relaxing
sleeping
traveling
working

1. Ben spends 8 hours working.

2. He spends 7 hours sleeping.

3. He spends 4 hours traveling.

4. He spends 3 hours relaxing.

5. He spends 2 hours cooking and eating.

B Circle *True* or *False*.

1. Ben spends the most time sleeping.	True	(False)
2. He spends more time traveling than sleeping.	True	False
3. He spends the least time relaxing.	True	False
4. He spends less time sleeping than working.	True	False
5. He spends more time relaxing than traveling.	True	False

C Complete the chart with how many hours you do these things. Then make a pie chart about your average day. Use the back of this paper.

Working	
Sleeping	
Traveling	
Relaxing	
Cooking and eating	

Lesson **F** *Another view*

A Complete the pie chart. Use the information below.

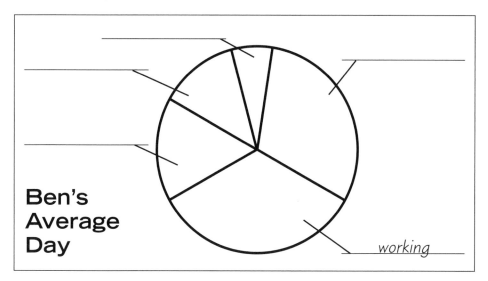

Ben's
Average
Day

working

1. Ben spends the most time working.

2. He spends the least time cooking and eating.

3. He spends almost as much time sleeping as working.

4. He spends more time traveling than relaxing.

B Circle *True* or *False*. Write two more true or false sentences about Ben.

1. Ben spends the most time sleeping.	True	(False)
2. He spends more time traveling than sleeping.	True	False
3. He spends the least time relaxing.	True	False
4. He spends less time sleeping than working.	True	False
5. He spends more time relaxing than traveling.	True	False
6. _____	True	False
7. _____	True	False

C Complete the chart with how many hours you do these things. Then make a pie chart about your average day. Use the back of this paper.

Working	
Sleeping	
Traveling	
Relaxing	
Cooking and eating	

Lesson **F** *Another view*

Name: _____

A Complete the pie chart. Use the information below.

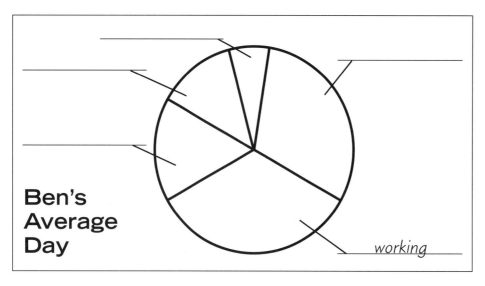

Ben's Average Day

working

1. Ben spends the most time working.

2. He spends the least time cooking and eating.

3. He spends almost as much time sleeping as working.

4. He spends more time traveling than relaxing.

B Complete the sentences. Write two more sentences about Ben.

1. Ben spends the most time ____*working*____ .

2. He spends more time _____ than sleeping.

3. He spends the least time _____ .

4. He spends less time sleeping than _____ .

5. He spends more time relaxing than _____ .

6. _____

7. _____

C Complete the chart with how many hours you do these things. Then make a pie chart about your average day. Use the back of this paper.

Working	
Sleeping	
Traveling	
Relaxing	
Cooking and eating	

Lesson A *Get ready*

A Circle the correct definition.

1. debt
   a. money that you can borrow
   b. money that you owe

2. interest
   a. the amount in your bank account
   b. the cost of borrowing money

3. balance
   a. money that you can borrow
   b. the amount in your bank account

4. to pay off
   a. to give back money that you owe
   b. the cost of borrowing money

5. loan
   a. money that you can borrow
   b. the amount in your bank account

B Match.

1. Why don't you like to borrow money? __c__

2. Why is it expensive to borrow money? ____

3. How much is in your bank account? ____

4. I don't have enough money to buy a car. ____

5. I'm trying to save money. ____

a. Because you have to pay interest.

b. Are you planning to pay off your loan?

c. Because I don't want to get into debt.

d. I'm not sure. I need to check my balance.

e. You could get a loan from the bank.

C Solve the problems.

1. Lenny borrowed $500 from the bank to pay for his car. He paid back $200 a year for three years. How much was the interest? $_____

   $200 × 3 = $600 $600 − $500 = _____

2. Le Than borrowed $2,000 from the bank to pay for her new computer. She paid back $100 per month for two years. How much was the interest? $_____

D Answer the questions.

1. When do people sometimes need a loan?

   _____

   _____

2. Why do some people get into debt?

   _____

   _____

A Match the words with their definitions.

1. debt _*d*_   a. the cost of borrowing money

2. interest _____   b. money that you can borrow

3. balance _____   c. to give back money that you owe

4. to pay off _____   d. money that you owe

5. loan _____   e. the amount in your bank account

B Complete the sentences. Use words from Exercise A.

1. **A** Why don't you like to borrow money?

   B Because I don't want to get into ____*debt*____ .

2. **A** Why is it expensive to borrow money?

   B Because you have to pay _____ .

3. **A** How much is in your bank account?

   B I'm not sure. I need to check my _____ .

4. **A** I don't have enough money to buy a car.

   B You could get a _____ from the bank.

5. **A** I'm trying to save money.

   B Are you planning to _____ your loan?

C Solve the problems.

1. Lenny borrowed $500 from the bank to pay for his car. He paid back
   $200 a year for three years. How much was the interest? $ _____

2. Le Than borrowed $2,000 from the bank to pay for her new computer.
   She paid back $100 per month for two years. How much was the
   interest? $ _____

3. Suri borrowed $1,600 from the bank to fix her roof. She paid back $300
   per month for 6 months. Then she still owed $50. How much was the
   interest? $ _____

D Answer the questions. Write two ideas for each question.

1. When do people sometimes need a loan? _____

   _____

2. Why do some people get into debt? _____

   _____

Lesson A Get ready

A Complete the words to match the definitions.

1. d_ebt_____: money that you owe

2. i_____: the cost of borrowing money

3. b_____: the amount in your bank account

4. to p_____ o_____: to give back money that you owe

5. l_____: money that you can borrow

B Write responses. Use words from Exercise A. Use other words if necessary.

1. **A** Why don't you like to borrow money?

   B Because I don't want to _get into debt_____ .

2. **A** Why is it expensive to borrow money?

   B Because you have to _____ .

3. **A** How much is in your bank account?

   B I'm not sure. I need to check _____ .

4. **A** I don't have enough money to buy a car.

   B You could _____ from the bank.

5. **A** I'm trying to save money.

   B Are you planning to _____ your loan?

C Solve the problems. Write one more problem.

1. Lenny borrowed $500 from the bank to pay for his car. He paid back $200 a year for three years. How much was the interest? $ _____

2. Le Than borrowed $2,000 from the bank to pay for her new computer. She paid back $100 per month for two years. How much was the interest? $ _____

3. Suri borrowed $1,600 from the bank to fix her roof. She paid back $300 per month for 6 months. Then she still owed $50. How much was the interest? $ _____

4. _____

   _____

D Answer the questions. Write two ideas for each question.

1. When do people sometimes need a loan? _____

   _____

2. Why do some people get into debt? _____

Lesson B Modals

A Match the pictures with the conversations.

_b_ 1. **A** What could I do for my wife's birthday?

   B You could bake a cake.

____ 2. **A** I want to save more money.

   B Why don't you cancel your credit cards?

____ 3. **A** I want to buy a car.

   B You could check the newspaper.

____ 4. **A** I want to sell my sofa.

   B You should advertise online.

B Complete the conversations. Choose a word from the box.

cell phone calls	clothes	food	rent

1. **A** I spend too much money on _cell phone calls_ .

   B You could get a cheaper calling plan.

2. **A** I spend too much money on _____ .

   B You could go to a thrift store. They have lots of different sizes and styles.

3. **A** I spend too much money on _____ .

   B You should find a cheaper apartment.

4. **A** I spend too much money on _____ .

   B You should compare food prices before you shop.

C What do you spend too much money on? Write a problem and a piece of advice for yourself.

I spend too much money on _____ .

I should _____ .

A Look at the pictures. Complete the conversations. Match them with the pictures.

| advertise online | bake a cake | cancel your credit cards | check the newspaper |

_b_ 1. **A** What could I do for my wife's birthday?

    B You could _bake a cake_____ .

_____ 2. **A** I want to save more money.

    B Why don't you _____ ?

_____ 3. **A** I want to buy a car.

    B You could _____ .

_____ 4. **A** I want to sell my sofa.

    B You should _____ .

B Complete the conversations. Guess the problems.

1. **A** I spend too much money on _cell phone calls_____ .

    B You could get a cheaper calling plan.

2. **A** I spend too much money on _____ .

    B You could go to a thrift store. They have lots of different sizes and styles.

3. **A** I spend too much money on _____ .

    B You should find a cheaper apartment.

4. **A** I spend too much money on _____ .

    B You should compare food prices before you shop.

C What do you spend too much money on? Write two problems and two pieces of advice for yourself.

1. I spend too much money on _____ . I should _____ .

2. I spend too much money on _____ . I should _____ .

Lesson B *Modals*

A Look at the pictures. Complete the conversations. Match them with the pictures.

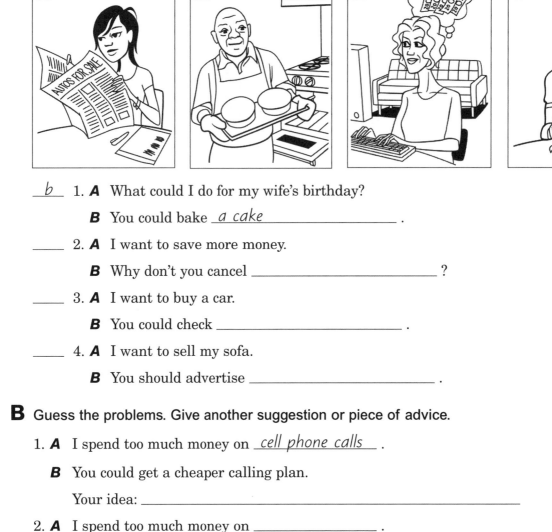

b 1. **A** What could I do for my wife's birthday?

   B You could bake *a cake* _____ .

____ 2. **A** I want to save more money.

   B Why don't you cancel _____ ?

____ 3. **A** I want to buy a car.

   B You could check _____ .

____ 4. **A** I want to sell my sofa.

   B You should advertise _____ .

B Guess the problems. Give another suggestion or piece of advice.

1. **A** I spend too much money on *cell phone calls* .

   B You could get a cheaper calling plan.

   Your idea: _____

2. **A** I spend too much money on _____ .

   B You could go to a thrift store. They have lots of different sizes and styles.

   Your idea: _____

3. **A** I spend too much money on _____ .

   B You should find a cheaper apartment.

   Your idea: _____

4. **A** I spend too much money on _____ .

   B You should compare food prices before you shop.

   Your idea: _____

C What do you spend too much money on? Write three problems and three pieces of advice for yourself. Use the back of this paper.

Name: _____

Lesson C *Gerunds*

A Circle the correct preposition.

1. I'm excited **of** / (**about**) starting school in the fall.

2. I'm afraid **of** / **about** losing my job.

3. I'm worried **in** / **about** paying my rent next month.

4. I'm happy **of** / **about** passing my exam last month.

5. I'm interested **in** / **about** learning about computers.

6. I'm tired **of** / **about** watching ads on TV.

B Complete the questions with the correct adjective.

afraid	excited	interested	worried

1. What are you ___*excited*___ about?   Starting a new job.

2. What are you _____ about?   Paying my bills.

3. What are you _____ of?   Failing my test.

4. What are you _____ in?   Buying a new TV.

C Correct the sentences. Add the missing word.

1. Denise ᵢₛ interested in buying a new car.   (is)

2. Francisco is afraid losing his credit card.   (of)

3. What you thinking about?   (are)

4. Are they worried paying their bills?   (about)

5. What are you afraid?   (of)

6. He's interested buying a used car.   (in)

D Answer the questions with information about yourself.

1. What are you happy about?

_____

2. What are you interested in?

_____

Name: _____

Lesson C Gerunds

A Complete the sentences with the correct preposition.

1. I'm excited ___*about*___ starting school in the fall.

2. I'm afraid _____ losing my job.

3. I'm worried _____ paying my rent next month.

4. I'm happy _____ passing my exam last month.

5. I'm interested _____ learning about computers.

6. I'm tired _____ watching ads on TV.

B Complete the questions with the correct adjective and preposition.

afraid	excited	interested	worried

about	about	in	of

1. What are you ___*excited about*___ ? Starting a new job.

2. What are you _____ ? Paying my bills.

3. What are you _____ ? Failing my test.

4. What are you _____ ? Buying a new TV.

C Correct the sentences. Add the missing word.

1. Denise ^is^ interested in buying a new car.

2. Francisco is afraid losing his credit card.

3. What you thinking about?

4. Are they worried paying their bills?

5. What are you afraid?

6. He's interested buying a used car.

D Answer the questions with information about yourself.

1. What are you happy about?

_____

2. What are you interested in?

_____

3. What are you tired of?

_____

Lesson C *Gerunds*

A Complete the sentences. Add the correct preposition and a verb from the box.

learn	pass	start
lose	pay	watch

1. I'm excited _____*about starting*_____ school in the fall.

2. I'm afraid _____ my job.

3. I'm worried _____ my rent next month.

4. I'm happy _____ my exam last month.

5. I'm interested _____ about computers.

6. I'm tired _____ ads on TV.

B Complete the questions with the correct adjective and preposition.

afraid	excited	interested	worried

1. What are you _____*excited about*_____ ?   Starting a new job.

2. What are you _____ ?   Paying my bills.

3. What are you _____ ?   Failing my test.

4. What are you _____ ?   Buying a new TV.

C Correct the sentences if necessary.

1. Denise ^*is* interested in buying a new car.

2. Francisco is afraid losing his credit card.

3. What are you thinking about?

4. Are they worried paying their bills?

5. What are you afraid?

6. He's interested in buying a used car.

D Answer the questions with information about yourself.

1. What are you happy about? _____

2. What are you interested in? _____

3. What are you tired of? _____

4. What are you worried about? _____

Lesson D Reading

A Read the article. Circle the correct answers.

Worried About Spending Too Much?

It's the end of the month, and suddenly you don't have enough money for the electric bill, the rent, or credit card payments. What can you do? Here are some tips if you are worried about spending too much.

First, write down your family budget. How much does your family spend each month on food, clothes, entertainment, and transportation? Then think of easy ways to spend less on each item. For example, you could try to buy some things at a thrift store. Another strategy is to compare prices online, especially if you are buying something large like a TV or computer. You could also look for coupons and discounts in the newspapers.

Some people spend too much because they use credit cards with high interest rates and only make the minimum payment. If you want to save money, use only one credit card. Or, use a debit card or cash instead. Then you will not be afraid of getting into debt.

---

1. The main idea of this article is _____ .
   a. how to spend money
   b.) how to save money
   c. how to use a credit card

2. *Write down your family budget* means _____ .
   a. make a list of your debts
   b. make a list of your savings
   c. make a list of your expenses

3. The article suggests three ways of _____ .
   a. buying better things
   b. controlling your spending
   c. paying off your debt

4. The article says that credit card bills are often high because _____ .
   a. people only pay the minimum
   b. people don't have too many cards
   c. people don't save money

B Look at the words in **bold**. Write *noun* or *adjective*.

1. Make a **family** budget. ___adjective___

2. I don't use a credit **card**. _____

3. What is the interest **rate**? _____

4. How much is the **minimum** payment? _____

C Do you have any tips for saving money? Write one tip.

_____

_____

A Read the article. Circle the correct answers.

> ## Worried About Spending Too Much?
>
> It's the end of the month, and suddenly you don't have enough money for the electric bill, the rent, or credit card payments. What can you do? Here are some tips if you are worried about spending too much.
>
> First, write down your family budget. How much does your family spend each month on food, clothes, entertainment, and transportation? Then think of easy ways to spend less on each item. For example, you could try to buy some things at a thrift store. Another strategy is to compare prices online, especially if you are buying something large like a TV or computer. You could also look for coupons and discounts in the newspapers.
>
> Some people spend too much because they use credit cards with high interest rates and only make the minimum payment. If you want to save money, use only one credit card. Or, use a debit card or cash instead. Then you will not be afraid of getting into debt.

1. The main idea of this article is _____ .
   a. how to spend money
   b. how to save money
   c. how to use a credit card
   d. how to pay off your debts

2. *Write down your family budget* means _____ .
   a. make a list of your debts
   b. make a list of your savings
   c. make a list of your expenses
   d. make a list of ways to save

3. The article suggests three ways of _____ .
   a. buying better things
   b. controlling your spending
   c. paying off your debt
   d. paying your bills

4. The article says that credit card bills are often high because _____ .
   a. people only pay the minimum
   b. people don't have too many cards
   c. people don't save money
   d. people use debit cards

B Underline the correct word in each sentence.

1. (an adjective) Make a <u>family</u> budget.

2. (a noun) I don't use a credit card.

3. (a noun) What is the interest rate?

4. (an adjective) How much is the minimum payment?

C Do you have any tips for saving money? Write two tips.

1. _____

2. _____

A Read the article. Complete the sentences.

Worried About Spending Too Much?

It's the end of the month, and suddenly you don't have enough money for the electric bill, the rent, or credit card payments. What can you do? Here are some tips if you are worried about spending too much.

First, write down your family budget. How much does your family spend each month on food, clothes, entertainment, and transportation? Then think of easy ways to spend less on each item. For example, you could try to buy some things at a thrift store. Another strategy is to compare prices online, especially if you are buying something large like a TV or computer. You could also look for coupons and discounts in the newspapers.

Some people spend too much because they use credit cards with high interest rates and only make the minimum payment. If you want to save money, use only one credit card. Or, use a debit card or cash instead. Then you will not be afraid of getting into debt.

---

1. The main idea of this article is _____ .
   a. how to spend money
   b. how to save money *(circled)*
   c. how to use a credit card
   d. how to pay off your debts

2. *Write down your family budget* means _____ .
   a. make a list of your debts
   b. make a list of your savings
   c. make a list of your expenses
   d. make a list of ways to save

3. The article suggests three ways of _____ .
   a. buying better things
   b. controlling your spending
   c. paying off your debt
   d. paying your bills

4. The article says that credit card bills are often high because _____ .
   a. people only pay the minimum
   b. people don't have too many cards
   c. people don't save money
   d. people use debit cards

B Underline the adjective and circle the noun in each sentence.

1. Make a <u>family</u> (budget).
2. I don't use a credit card.
3. What is the interest rate?
4. How much is the minimum payment?
5. Go to a thrift store.

C Do you have any tips for saving money? Write three tips on the back of this paper.

Lesson **E** *Writing*

A Complete the letters.

| afford | bought | car | cell phone | clothes | need |

1. Dear Money Man,

    We bought a new ____*car*____ two months ago, but now it is very

difficult for us to make the payments. Gas prices have gone up and we cannot

_____ the gas. We are driving my old car because it uses less gas. What

should we do?

    Two-car Dad

2. Dear Money Man,

    My daughter spends too much time on her _____ . She talks to her

friends all day and all night. I _____ it for her because I can contact her

any time, but the phone bills are too high! What should I do?

    Worried Mom

3. Dear Money Man,

    I go to the mall every weekend, and I always buy new _____ for

myself. I don't really _____ them and I can't afford them. I have bags

of new clothes in my closet. I never wear them, but I'm too shy to take them

back to the store. What should I do?

    Clothes Crazy

B Match the letters from Exercise A with the advice.

    _2_ You should give her a phone budget.

    ____ You should stop going to the mall.

    ____ You should exchange your car.

C Choose one of the letters from Exercise A and write a reply.

Dear _____ ,

    It's important to have _____ , but you don't need to spend all

your money on it / them. I have a few suggestions. First, you could

_____ .

Next, you could _____ .

Finally, you could _____ .

    Money Man

Lesson **E** *Writing*

A Complete the letters.

afford	car	cell phone	clothes	high	payments

1. Dear Money Man,

   We bought a new ____car____ two months ago, but now it is very difficult
   for us to make the _____ . Gas prices have gone up and we cannot afford
   the gas. We are driving my old car because it uses less gas. What should we do?

   Two-car Dad

2. Dear Money Man,

   My daughter spends too much time on her _____ . She talks to her
   friends all day and all night. I bought it for her because I can contact her any time,
   but the phone bills are too _____ ! What should I do?

   Worried Mom

3. Dear Money Man,

   I go to the mall every weekend, and I always buy new _____ for
   myself. I don't really need them and I can't _____ them. I have bags of
   new clothes in my closet. I never wear them, but I'm too shy to take them back to
   the store. What should I do?

   Clothes Crazy

B Match the letters from Exercise A with the advice.

_2_ You should give her a phone budget.   ____ You should cancel your credit cards.

____ You should stop going to the mall.   ____ You should sell your new car.

____ You should exchange your car.   ____ Your daughter should pay her own phone bills.

C Choose one of the letters from Exercise A and write a reply.

Dear _____ ,

   It's important to have _____ , but you don't need to spend all
your money on it / them. I have a few suggestions. First, _____

_____ .

Next, _____ .

Finally, _____ .

   Money Man

Lesson E **Writing**

A Complete the letters.

| afford | car | cell phone | clothes | difficult | high | payments | spends | wear |

1. Dear Money Man,

   We bought a new ____car____ two months ago, but now it is very _____ for us
   to make the _____ . Gas prices have gone up and we cannot afford the gas. We are
   driving my old car because it uses less gas. What should we do?

   Two-car Dad

2. Dear Money Man,

   My daughter _____ too much time on her _____ . She talks to her
   friends all day and all night. I bought it for her because I can contact her any time, but the
   phone bills are too _____ ! What should I do?

   Worried Mom

3. Dear Money Man,

   I go to the mall every weekend, and I always buy new _____ for myself. I don't
   really need them and I can't _____ them. I have bags of new clothes in my closet. I
   never _____ them, but I'm too shy to take them back to the store. What should I do?

   Clothes Crazy

B Write one piece of advice or a suggestion for each letter from Exercise A.
Use *should* or *could*.

1. _____

2. _____

3. _____

C Choose one of the letters from Exercise A and write a reply. Use *First*,
Next, and *Finally*.

Dear _____ ,

   It's important to have _____ , but you don't need to spend all
your money on it / them. I have a few ideas for you. _____

_____

_____

_____

   Money Man

Lesson F *Another view*

A Look at the chart. Which car dealer should each person choose? Write *Ace* or *Star.*

Car Loans		
	Ace Car Dealer	Star Car Dealer
Amount of loan	Up to $21,000	Up to $15,000
Years to pay	3–7 years	1–5 years
Interest rate	14%	11%

1. Dave wants to pay off his car loan in seven years. _____*Ace*_____

2. Lila wants a low interest rate on her car loan. _____

3. Stan needs to borrow $18,000 to buy his new car. _____

4. Susanna plans to pay off her car loan in just one year. _____

5. Drew doesn't want to pay more than 12 percent interest on his car loan. _____

6. Patty plans to pay off her car loan in six years. _____

B Complete the chart with the information below.

1. I like to eat out.
2. I pay cash for everything.
3. I use more than two credit cards.
4. I spend a lot of time on the phone.
5. I save money in the bank every month.
6. I make the minimum credit card payment.
7. I compare prices online.
8. I use coupons to get a discount.

This person spends a lot of money.	This person saves a lot of money.
I like to eat out.	

Lesson **F** *Another View*

A Look at the chart. Which car dealer should each person choose? Write *Ace* or *Star*.

Car Loans		
	Ace Car Dealer	Star Car Dealer
Amount of loan	Up to $21,000	Up to $15,000
Years to pay	3–7 years	1–5 years
Interest rate	14%	11%

1. Dave wants to pay off his car loan in seven years. _____*Ace*_____

2. Lila wants a low interest rate on her car loan. _____

3. Stan needs to borrow $18,000 to buy his new car. _____

4. Susanna plans to pay off her car loan in just one year. _____

5. Drew doesn't want to pay more than 12 percent interest on his car loan. _____

6. Patty plans to pay off her car loan in six years. _____

7. Lauren needs to borrow $10,000 for her new car. She wants to pay off the loan in four years, and she wants a low interest rate. _____

B Complete the chart with the information below.

1. I like to eat out.

2. I pay cash for everything.

3. I use more than two credit cards.

4. I spend a lot of time on the phone.

5. I save money in the bank every month.

6. I make the minimum credit card payment.

7. I compare prices online.

8. I like to buy new clothes every week.

9. I use coupons to get a discount.

10. I only buy things on sale.

This person spends a lot of money.	This person saves a lot of money.
I like to eat out.	

A Look at the chart. Which car dealer should each person choose? Write *Ace* or *Star.*

Car Loans		
	Ace Car Dealer	Star Car Dealer
Amount of loan	Up to $21,000	Up to $15,000
Years to pay	3–7 years	1–5 years
Interest rate	14%	11%

1. Dave wants to pay off his car loan in seven years. _____*Ace*_____

2. Lila wants a low interest rate on her car loan. _____

3. Stan needs to borrow $18,000 to buy his new car. _____

4. Susanna plans to pay off her car loan in just one year. _____

5. Drew doesn't want to pay more than 12 percent interest on his car loan. _____

6. Patty plans to pay off her car loan in six years. _____

7. Lauren needs to borrow $10,000 for her new car. She wants to pay off the loan in four years, and she wants a low interest rate. _____

8. Joe needs a loan of $14,000 for his new car. He needs to keep his monthly payments low, so he wants a long time to pay off the loan. _____

B Complete the chart with the information below. Add two ideas of your own.

1. I like to eat out.
2. I pay cash for everything.
3. I use more than two credit cards.
4. I spend a lot of time on the phone.
5. I save money in the bank every month.
6. I make the minimum credit card payment.
7. I compare prices online.
8. I like to buy new clothes every week.
9. I use coupons to get a discount.
10. I only buy things on sale.

This person spends a lot of money.	This person saves a lot of money.
I like to eat out.	

Lesson A *Get ready*

A Complete the interview. Then read the interview with a partner.

Pleased to meet you.
I'm working in an Internet sales company.
Thank you.
For about a year.
I prefer the day shift.
I'm applying for the job of sales manager.

Manager Good morning. Please come in and sit down.

Claudia *Thank you.* _____

Manager My name is Andrew Gladstone. I'm the personnel manager.

Claudia _____

Manager Which job are you applying for?

Claudia _____

Manager I see. And what is your current job?

Claudia _____

Manager How long have you been working there?

Claudia _____

Manager Which shift do you prefer?

Claudia _____

B Continue the interview. Circle the best response.

1. **Manager** Tell me about your background.

   Claudia a. I speak Portuguese. (b.) I am from Brazil. c. I get along with others.

2. **Manager** What are your strengths?

   Claudia a. I am reliable. b. I want to be a manager. c. I'm studying English.

3. **Manager** What skills do you have?

   Claudia a. I want to be a manager. b. I have some sales experience. c. I studied computers.

Lesson A Get ready

A Number the interview in the correct order. Then read the interview with a partner.

_____ For about a year.

_____ My name is Andrew Gladstone. I'm the personnel manager.

_____ Pleased to meet you.

_1_ Good morning. Please come in and sit down.

_____ Which job are you applying for?

_____ Which shift do you prefer?

_____ Thank you.

_____ I'm working in an Internet sales company.

_12_ I prefer the day shift.

_____ How long have you been working there?

_____ I'm applying for the job of sales manager.

_____ I see. And what is your current job?

B Continue the interview. Use the information below.

> Claudia is from Brazil. She speaks Portuguese. She's a very reliable person. She gets along well with others. She wants to be a manager. She has some sales experience. She studied computers. She is studying English now.

Manager Tell me about your background.

Claudia _I am from Brazil._ _____

Manager What are your strengths?

Claudia _____

Manager What skills do you have?

Claudia _____

A Complete the interview. Use the information in the article. Then read the interview with a partner.

> Claudia is from Brazil. She speaks Portuguese. She's applying for the job of sales manager. She's a very reliable person. She gets along well with others. She is working in an Internet sales company right now. She has been working there for about a year. She wants to be a manager. She has some sales experience. She studied computers. She is studying English now. She prefers the day shift.

Manager Good morning. Please come in and sit down.

Claudia *Thank you.* _____

Manager My name is Andrew Gladstone. I'm the personnel manager.

Claudia _____

Manager Which job are you applying for?

Claudia _____

Manager I see. And what is your current job?

Claudia _____

Manager How long have you been working there?

Claudia _____

Manager Which shift do you prefer?

Claudia _____

B Continue the interview. Use the information in the article. Use your own ideas to end the interview.

Manager Tell me about your background.

Claudia _____

Manager What are your strengths?

Claudia _____

Manager What skills do you have?

Claudia _____

Manager _____

Claudia _____

Lesson B *Present perfect continuous*

A Put the time phrases in the correct column.

two days	three years	July 12th	2002
3:00 p.m.	September	a long time	an hour

for	*since*
two days	

B Rewrite the sentences so they have the same meaning.

1. I started working here six weeks ago.

   I _*have been working here*_____ for six weeks.

2. We started using computers five years ago.

   We _____ for five years.

3. Rick started looking for a job in July.

   Rick _____ since July.

4. Serena started studying art in 2004.

   Serena _____ since 2004.

5. Tina and Tam started fixing the car three hours ago.

   Tina and Tam _____ for three hours.

6. You started talking on the phone 40 minutes ago.

   You _____ for 40 minutes.

C Correct the sentences. Add the missing word.

1. How long you been working here?   (have)
   have ^

2. Have you waiting for a long time?   (been)

3. We been painting this house since Monday.   (have)

4. Has Tran been studying a long time?   (for)

5. How have we been waiting here?   (long)

6. Denis and Jean have talking all morning.   (been)

Lesson B *Present perfect continuous*

A Put the time phrases in the correct column.

two days	three years	July 12th	2002	five hours	ten weeks
3:00 p.m.	September	a long time	an hour	yesterday	Friday

for		*since*	
two days			

B Rewrite the sentences so they have the same meaning.

1. I started working here six weeks ago.

   I _have been working here_ for _six weeks_ .

2. We started using computers five years ago.

   We _____ for _____ .

3. Rick started looking for a job in July.

   Rick _____ since _____ .

4. Serena started studying art in 2004.

   Serena _____ since _____ .

5. Tina and Tam started fixing the car three hours ago.

   Tina and Tam _____ for _____ .

6. You started talking on the phone 40 minutes ago.

   You _____ for _____ .

C Correct the sentences. Add the missing word from the box.

been	been	for	have	have	long

1. How long ʌ*have* you been working here?

2. Have you waiting for a long time?

3. We been painting this house since Monday.

4. Has Tran been studying a long time?

5. How have we been waiting here?

6. Denis and Jean have talking all morning.

Name: _____

Lesson B *Present perfect continuous*

A Put the time phrases in the correct column. Add two more time phrases.

| two days | three years | July 12th | 2002 | five hours | ten weeks | a month |
| 3:00 p.m. | September | a long time | an hour | yesterday | Friday | this morning |

for			*since*	
two days				

B Rewrite the sentences so they have the same meaning. Use the present perfect continuous.

1. I started working here six weeks ago.

   I have been working here for six weeks.

2. We started using computers five years ago.

   _____

3. Rick started looking for a job in July.

   _____

4. Serena started studying art in 2004.

   _____

5. Tina and Tam started fixing the car three hours ago.

   _____

6. You started talking on the phone 40 minutes ago.

   _____

C Correct the sentences. Add the missing word.

1. How long ^have you been working here?

2. Have you waiting for a long time?

3. We been painting this house since Monday.

4. Has Tran been studying a long time?

5. How have we been waiting here?

6. Denis and Jean have talking all morning.

Name: _____

Lesson C *Phrasal verbs*

A Complete the sentences with the correct pronouns.

1. Victor is going to throw out some papers.

   Victor is going to throw __*them*__ out.

2. The teacher is handing out the homework.

   The teacher is handing _____ out.

3. I am going to call my sister back.

   I am going to call _____ back.

4. Alex is turning off the lights.

   Alex is turning _____ off.

5. We are going to clean up the kitchen.

   We are going to clean _____ up.

6. Can you please turn up the TV?

   Can you please turn _____ up?

B Match two nouns with each phrasal verb.

a form	a job application	old newspapers	the kitchen	the TV
a friend	a relative	the classroom	the music	trash

1. call back   __*a friend, a relative*_____

2. throw away   _____

3. clean up   _____

4. turn down   _____

5. fill out   _____

C Complete the sentences using a phrasal verb and a pronoun.

1. You don't need the dictionary. Please put ___*it*___ ___*away*___ .

2. The kitchen is dirty. Please clean _____ _____ .

3. The TV is too loud. Please turn _____ _____ .

4. Your brother called this morning. Please call _____ _____ .

5. You don't need these old shoes. Please throw _____ _____ .

6. Here is the application. Please fill _____ _____ .

A Complete the sentences. Use pronouns.

1. Victor is going to throw out some papers.

   Victor is going to throw __them__ __out__ .

2. The teacher is handing out the homework.

   The teacher is handing _____ _____ .

3. I am going to call my sister back.

   I am going to call _____ _____ .

4. Alex is turning off the lights.

   Alex is turning _____ _____ .

5. We are going to clean up the kitchen.

   We are going to clean _____ _____ .

6. Can you please turn up the TV?

   Can you please turn _____ _____ ?

B Match three nouns with each phrasal verb.

a broken cup	a job application	my husband	the house	the TV
a form	a relative	old newspapers	the kitchen	the volume
a friend	a work order	the classroom	the music	trash

1. call back   __a friend, a relative. my husband__ _____

2. throw away   _____

3. clean up   _____

4. turn down   _____

5. fill out   _____

C Complete the sentences using a phrasal verb and a pronoun.

call	clean	fill	put	throw	turn

1. You don't need the dictionary. Please __put it away__ _____ .

2. The kitchen is dirty. Please _____ .

3. The TV is too loud. Please _____ .

4. Your brother called this morning. Please _____ .

5. You don't need these old shoes. Please _____ .

6. Here is the application. Please _____ .

Lesson **C** *Phrasal verbs*

Name: _____

A Rewrite the sentences. Use pronouns.

1. Victor is going to throw out some papers.

   Victor is going to throw them out. _____

2. The teacher is handing out the homework.

   _____

3. I am going to call my sister back.

   _____

4. Alex is turning off the lights.

   _____

5. We are going to clean up the kitchen.

   _____

6. Can you please turn up the TV?

   _____

B Match four nouns with each phrasal verb.

a broken cup	a relative	old newspapers	the heat	the music
a form	a survey	old shoes	the house	the TV
a friend	a work order	the classroom	the kitchen	the volume
a job application	my husband	the doctor	the lunchroom	trash

1. call back   *a friend, a relative, my husband, the doctor* _____

2. throw away   _____

3. clean up   _____

4. turn down   _____

5. fill out   _____

C Complete the sentences using a phrasal verb and a pronoun.

1. You don't need the dictionary. Please _put it away_____ .

2. The kitchen is dirty. Please _____ .

3. The TV is too loud. Please _____ .

4. Your brother called this morning. Please _____ .

5. You don't need these old shoes. Please _____ .

6. Here is the application. Please _____ .

A Match the words to the definitions.

1. critical __c__   a. to get to know other people

2. to network _____   b. a gathering or conference

3. a fair _____   c. very important

4. patient _____   d. very strong

5. firm _____   e. a belief in yourself

6. confidence _____   f. calm or uncomplaining

B Read the blog. Complete the text. Use the words from Exercise A.

Ana's Blog

Sunday: Tomorrow I start my new job! I'm going to keep a blog because I want to remember how I felt when I began working. The first days in a new job are usually _____*critical*_____ , and I want to be successful. I hope it goes well.
              1

Monday: Today was very exciting! The manager greeted me with a _____ handshake and gave me a tour of the office. I had lunch with my new co-workers. I felt
                                                                                              2
shy and didn't say much. I know it's important to _____ with everyone at work,
                                                                          3
so I've been trying to show _____ .
                                                    4

Tuesday: Today was my second day. Everything was confusing. My job seems very different from what they told me at the job _____ . I have been asking a lot of questions. I'm
                                                              5
not sure if this is the right job for me, but I know I need to be _____ .
                                                                                        6

C Circle the correct answers.

1. Ana has been keeping a blog because _____ .
   a. she wants to remember this time
   b. she wants her friends to read it
   c. she has a lot of problems

2. Ana tried to show confidence because _____ .
   a. she was confused about her job
   b. she was with her co-workers
   c. she went to a restaurant

3. Ana was confused because _____ .
   a. she didn't know anyone there
   b. her job wasn't what they told her
   c. she went to the wrong company

4. Ana has been asking questions because _____ .
   a. she wants to network
   b. she doesn't have any friends
   c. she's not sure about the job

Name: _____

Lesson D *Reading*

A Complete the words to match the definitions.

1. c _r_ _i_ _t_ _i_ _c_ _a_ _l_ : very important

2. to n __ __ __ __ __ __ : to get to know other people

3. a f __ __ __ : a gathering or conference

4. p __ __ __ __ __ __ : calm or uncomplaining

5. f __ __ __ : very strong

6. c __ __ __ __ __ __ __ __ : a belief in yourself

B Read the blog. Complete the text. Use the words from Exercise A.

Ana's Blog

Sunday: Tomorrow I start my new job! I'm going to keep a blog because I want to remember how I felt when I began working. The first days in a new job are usually ___*critical*___ , and I want to be successful. I hope it goes well.
                    1

Monday: Today was very exciting! The manager greeted me with a _____ handshake and gave me a tour of the office. I had lunch with my new co-workers. I felt
                    2
shy and didn't say much. I know it's important to _____ with everyone at work,
                    3
so I've been trying to show _____ .
                    4

Tuesday: Today was my second day. Everything was confusing. My job seems very different from what they told me at the job _____ . I have been asking a lot of questions. I'm
                    5
not sure if this is the right job for me, but I know I need to be _____ .
                    6

C Circle the correct answers.

1. Ana has been keeping a blog because ____ .
   a. she wants to remember this time
   b. she wants her friends to read it
   c. she has a lot of problems
   d. it's a part of her job duties

2. Ana tried to show confidence because ____ .
   a. she was confused about her job
   b. she was with her co-workers
   c. she went to a restaurant
   d. she likes her new job

3. Ana was confused because ____ .
   a. she didn't know anyone there
   b. her job wasn't what they told her
   c. she went to the wrong company
   d. her manager shook her hand

4. Ana has been asking questions because ____ .
   a. she wants to network
   b. she doesn't have any friends
   c. she's not sure about the job
   d. she is very patient

Lesson D Reading

A Write the words to match the definitions.

1. c<u>ritical</u> _____ : very important

2. to n_____ : to get to know other people

3. a f_____ : a gathering or conference

4. p_____ : calm or uncomplaining

5. f_____ : very strong

6. c_____ : a belief in yourself

B Read the blog. Complete the text. Use the words from Exercise A.

Ana's Blog

Sunday: Tomorrow I start my new job! I'm going to keep a blog because I want to remember how I felt when I began working. The first days in a new job are usually ___<u>critical</u>___ and I want to be successful. I hope it goes well.
1

Monday: Today was very exciting! The manager greeted me with a _____ handshake and gave me a tour of the office. I had lunch with my new co-workers. I felt
2
shy and didn't say much. I know it's important to _____ with everyone at work,
3
so I've been trying to show _____ .
4

Tuesday: Today was my second day. Everything was confusing. My job seems very different from what they told me at the job _____ . I have been asking a lot of questions. I'm
5
not sure if this is the right job for me, but I know I need to be _____ .
6

C Answer the questions.

1. Why has Ana been keeping a blog?

_____

2. Why has Ana been trying to show confidence?

_____

3. Why was Ana confused about her job?

_____

4. Why has Ana been asking questions?

_____

Lesson E *Writing*

A Number these items in the correct order for writing a thank-you letter.

_____ Your name   _____ Sincerely,

_1_ Your address   _____ Signature

_____ The name of the person you are writing to   _____ Dear . . .

_____ The reason you are writing   _____ The date

_____ The address of the person you are writing to

B Read the thank-you letter. Match the information in the letter with the correct number.

> ❶ ⌈ 48 South Street
>   ⌊ Albany, NY 12224
> ❷ June 26, 2008
>
> ❸ Andrew Gladstone, Personnel Manager
>   SmartZone Department Store
> ❹⌈ 1564 Central Ave.
>   ⌊ Albany, NY 12210
>
> Dear Mr. Gladstone:
>   I would like to thank you for the job interview I had with you on June 25. I appreciate the time you spent with me. Thank you for giving me information about the job of sales manager. It sounds very interesting.
>   Thank you again for your time. I hope to hear from you soon.
>
>   Sincerely,
>   ❺ *Claudia Silva*
>   ❻ Claudia Silva

_4_ The address of the person the letter is for

_____ The name of the person who wrote the letter

_____ The date

_____ The name of the person the letter is for

_____ The signature

_____ The address of the person who wrote the letter

A Number these items in the correct order for writing a thank-you letter.

____ Your name   ____ The address of the person you are writing to

_1_ Your address   ____ Sincerely,

____ The name of the person you are writing to   ____ Signature

     ____ Dear . . .

____ The reason you are writing   ____ The date

B Use the information below to complete the thank-you letter.

Claudia Silva is going to write a thank-you letter to Mr. Andrew Gladstone, the Personnel Manager of SmartZone Department Store. Claudia's address is 48 South Street, Albany, NY 12224. Mr. Gladstone's address is SmartZone Department Store, 1564 Central Avenue, Albany, NY 12210. Claudia attended an interview on June 25. Today's date is June 26, 2008. She wants to thank Mr. Gladstone for giving her information about the job of sales manager.

48 South Street
Albany, NY 12224
_____

_____ , Personnel Manager
SmartZone Department Store
1564 Central Ave.
Albany, NY 12210

Dear _____ :

     I would like to thank you for the job interview I had with you on

_____ . I appreciate the time you spent with me. Thank you for

_____ . It

sounds very interesting.

     Thank you again for your time. I hope to hear from you soon.

_____ ,

Claudia Silva
Claudia Silva

Lesson **E** *Writing*

A Number these items in the correct order for writing a thank-you letter.

_____ Your name

__1__ Your address

_____ The name of the person
you are writing to

_____ The reason you are writing

_____ The address of the person you are writing to

_____ Sincerely,

_____ Signature

_____ Dear . . .

_____ The date

B Use the information below to write a thank-you letter.

Claudia Silva is going to write a thank-you letter to Mr. Andrew Gladstone, the Personnel Manager of SmartZone Department Store. Claudia's address is 48 South Street, Albany, NY 12224. Mr. Gladstone's address is SmartZone Department Store, 1564 Central Avenue, Albany, NY 12210. Claudia attended an interview on June 25. Today's date is June 26, 2008. She wants to thank Mr. Gladstone for giving her information about the job of sales manager. She thinks it sounds very interesting.

Lesson F *Another view*

☑ ■ ■

A Look at the chart. Circle *True* or *False*.

> **Customer service manager** needed for busy
> department store in shopping mall. Must be
> patient, friendly, and a good time manager.

	Martin	Rosita
1. Did the applicant have good eye contact?	(1) 2 3 4 5	1 2 3 (4) 5
2. Did the applicant speak slowly and clearly?	1 2 3 (4) 5	1 (2) 3 4 5
3. Was the applicant enthusiastic?	1 (2) 3 4 5	1 2 (3) 4 5
4. What are the applicant's personal strengths?	Friendly and outgoing, enjoys talking with people	Intelligent, asks good questions
5. Do you think the applicant should get the job?	(Yes)/ No	Yes /(No)
Key: 1 = excellent 2 = very good 3 = good 4 = OK 5 = weak		

1. Martin has better eye contact than Rosita.   (True)   False

2. Martin speaks more slowly and clearly than Rosita.   True   False

3. Rosita is more enthusiastic than Martin.   True   False

4. Martin needs to improve his speaking.   True   False

5. Rosita needs to improve her eye contact.   True   False

6. The interviewer thinks Rosita should get the job.   True   False

B Match the questions with Martin's answers.

1. What job are you applying for? _d_

2. What is your current job? _____

3. What skills do you have? _____

4. Why should I hire you? _____

a. I can use a computer and I speak three languages.

b. Because I'm friendly and outgoing, and I love working with people.

c. I'm working as a hotel desk clerk.

d. I'm applying for the job of customer service manager.

Name: _____

Lesson F *Another view*

A Look at the chart. Circle the correct answers.

> **Customer service manager** needed for busy department store in shopping mall. Must be patient, friendly, and a good time manager.

	Martin	Rosita
1. Did the applicant have good eye contact?	① 2 3 4 5	1 2 3 ④ 5
2. Did the applicant speak slowly and clearly?	1 2 3 ④ 5	1 ② 3 4 5
3. Was the applicant enthusiastic?	1 ② 3 4 5	1 2 ③ 4 5
4. What are the applicant's personal strengths?	Friendly and outgoing, enjoys talking with people	Intelligent, asks good questions
5. Do you think the applicant should get the job?	ⓨes / No	Yes / ⓝo
Key: 1 = excellent 2 = very good 3 = good 4 = OK 5 = weak		

1. Martin _____ than Rosita.
   a. has better eye contact
   b. speaks more slowly and clearly
   c. is less enthusiastic

2. Rosita _____ than Martin.
   a. has better eye contact
   b. speaks more slowly and clearly
   c. is more enthusiastic

3. Martin _____ than Rosita.
   a. asks better questions
   b. speaks more slowly and clearly
   c. is more enthusiastic

4. Martin needs to improve his _____ .
   a. eye contact
   b. speaking
   c. enthusiasm

5. Rosita needs to improve her _____ .
   a. speaking
   b. intelligence
   c. eye contact

6. The interviewer thinks _____ should get the job.
   a. Martin
   b. Rosita
   c. both Martin and Rosita

B Write questions for Martin's answers.

1. *What job are you applying for?*

   I'm applying for the job of customer service manager.

2. _____

   I'm working as a hotel desk clerk.

3. _____

   I can use a computer and I speak three languages.

4. _____

   Because I'm friendly and outgoing, and I love working with people.

Lesson F *Another view*

Name: _____

A Look at the chart. Write the answers.

> **Customer service manager** needed for busy department store in shopping mall. Must be patient, friendly, and a good time manager.

	Martin	**Rosita**
1. Did the applicant have good eye contact?	① 2 3 4 5	1 2 3 ④ 5
2. Did the applicant speak slowly and clearly?	1 2 3 ④ 5	1 ② 3 4 5
3. Was the applicant enthusiastic?	1 ② 3 4 5	1 2 ③ 4 5
4. What are the applicant's personal strengths?	Friendly and outgoing, enjoys talking with people	Intelligent, asks good questions
5. Do you think the applicant should get the job?	Yes / No	Yes / No
Key: 1 = excellent 2 = very good 3 = good 4 = OK 5 = weak		

1. Who has better eye contact? *Martin has better eye contact than Rosita.*

2. Who speaks more slowly and clearly? _____

3. Who is more enthusiastic? _____

4. What does Martin need to improve? _____

5. What does Rosita need to improve? _____

6. Who does the interviewer think should get the job? _____

B Write questions for Martin's answers.

1. *What job are you applying for?*

   I'm applying for the job of customer service manager.

2. _____

   I'm working as a hotel desk clerk.

3. _____

   I can use a computer and I speak three languages.

4. _____

   Because I'm friendly and outgoing, and I love working with people.

Lesson A Get ready

A Complete the text in the flyer.

| broke into | crime | neighborhood | stole |

Join the Neighborhood Watch

Dear Neighbors,

Are you worried about crime in our _neighborhood_ ? Join our Neighborhood Watch and help make our neighborhood safer. Here are stories from some of our neighbors.

- "Some people _____ our garage while we were on vacation last summer and _____ our car."
- "Someone robbed my grocery store and took all the cash from the safe."
- "Robbers got in through the bathroom window. They stole our computer, TV, and DVD player."
- "Someone wrote graffiti on the front of my home and threw trash into the garden. Now I have to clean up the mess."

We all know that our neighborhood is getting more dangerous. Help us to reduce _____ . Join the Neighborhood Watch! Call 555-6726 to find out more.

B Match the questions and the answers.

1. What did robbers steal from the garage? _c_

2. What did someone take from the grocery store? _____

3. How did robbers get into one home? _____

4. What are the neighbors worried about? _____

5. What should the neighbors do? _____

a. They should join the Neighborhood Watch.

b. They got in through the bathroom window.

c. They stole a car.

d. Someone took all the cash.

e. They're worried about crime in the neighborhood.

C Write one way to make your neighborhood safer.

_____

Lesson A *Get ready*

A Complete the text in the flyer.

| broke into | crime | mess | neighborhood | robbed | stole |

Join the Neighborhood Watch

Dear Neighbors,

   Are you worried about crime in our <u>neighborhood</u> ? Join our Neighborhood Watch and help make our neighborhood safer. Here are stories from some of our neighbors.

- "Some people _____ our garage while we were on vacation last summer and _____ our car."
- "Someone _____ my grocery store and took all the cash from the safe."
- "Robbers got in through the bathroom window. They stole our computer, TV, and DVD player."
- "Someone wrote graffiti on the front of my home and threw trash into the garden. Now I have to clean up the _____ ."

   We all know that our neighborhood is getting more dangerous. Help us to reduce _____ . Join the Neighborhood Watch! Call 555-6726 to find out more.

B Answer the questions. Use the information in Exercise A.

1. What did robbers steal from the garage? *They stole a car.* _____

2. What did someone take from the grocery store? _____

3. How did robbers get into one home? _____

4. What are the neighbors worried about? _____

_____

5. What should the neighbors do? _____

_____

C Write two ways to make your neighborhood safer.

1. _____

_____

2. _____

_____

A Complete the text in the flyer.

broke into	got in	neighborhood	stole
crime	mess	robbed	

Join the Neighborhood Watch

Dear Neighbors,

   Are you worried about crime in our *neighborhood* ? Join our Neighborhood Watch and help make our neighborhood safer. Here are stories from some of our neighbors.

- "Some people _____ our garage while we were on vacation last summer and _____ our car."
- "Someone _____ my grocery store and took all the cash from the safe."
- "Robbers got in through the bathroom window. They _____ our computer, TV, and DVD player."
- "Someone wrote graffiti on the front of my home and threw trash into the garden. Now I have to clean up the _____ ."

   We all know that our neighborhood is getting more dangerous. Help us to reduce _____ . Join the Neighborhood Watch! Call 555-6726 to find out more.

B Write a question for each answer. Use the information in Exercise A.

1. What / robbers / steal / garage? *What did robbers steal from the garage?* _____
   They stole a car.

2. What / someone / take / grocery store? _____
   Someone took all the cash.

3. How / robbers / get / one home? _____
   They got in through the bathroom window.

4. What / neighbors / worried? _____
   They're worried about crime in their neighborhood.

5. What / neighbors / do? _____
   They should join the Neighborhood Watch.

C Write three ways to make your neighborhood safer. Use the back of this paper.

Lesson B Past continuous

A What were these people doing at 7:00 p.m. last night? Match the questions and the answers.

I was cooking dinner.

I was reading the paper.

I was e-mailing my friends.

I was talking on the phone.

We were babysitting our grandchildren.

Tina   Frank   Pauline   Dino   Sam   Luisa

1. Was Tina cooking dinner? __d__

2. What was Dino doing? ____

3. Was Frank talking on the phone? ____

4. What was Pauline doing? ____

5. Were Sam and Luisa cooking dinner? ____

6. What were Sam and Luisa doing? ____

a. He was talking on the phone.

b. They were babysitting.

c. No, they weren't.

d. Yes, she was.

e. She was e-mailing her friends.

f. No, he wasn't.

B Correct the mistakes.

1. What <u>Beth was</u> doing yesterday morning?

2. Teresa and Jimmy <u>was</u> watching TV all day.

3. I was <u>talk</u> with my friend on Monday night.

4. Was he <u>writting</u> a letter?

5. What <u>was</u> you wearing yesterday?

6. I <u>were</u> baking a cake for my daughter.

C What were you doing at each of these times yesterday?

Example: 7:00 a.m. _I was sleeping._

7:00 a.m.	
9:00 a.m.	
noon	
3:00 p.m.	
6:00 p.m.	
10:00 p.m.	

Name: _____

Lesson **B** *Past continuous*

A What were these people doing at 7:00 p.m. last night? Answer the questions.

I was cooking dinner.

I was reading the paper.

I was e-mailing my friends.

I was talking on the phone.

We were babysitting our grandchildren.

Tina **Frank** **Pauline** **Dino** **Sam** **Luisa**

1. Was Tina cooking dinner? *Yes, she was.* _____

2. What was Dino doing? _____

3. Was Frank talking on the phone? _____

4. What was Pauline doing? _____

5. Were Sam and Luisa cooking dinner? _____

6. What were Sam and Luisa doing? _____

B Correct the mistakes.

1. What Beth was doing yesterday morning?

2. Teresa and Jimmy was watching TV all day.

3. I was talk with my friend on Monday night.

4. Was he writting a letter?

5. What was you wearing yesterday?

6. I were baking a cake for my daughter.

C What were you doing at each of these times yesterday?

Example: 7:00 a.m. *I was sleeping.*

7:00 a.m.	
9:00 a.m.	
noon	
3:00 p.m.	
6:00 p.m.	
10:00 p.m.	

A What were these people doing at 7:00 p.m. last night? Complete and answer the questions.

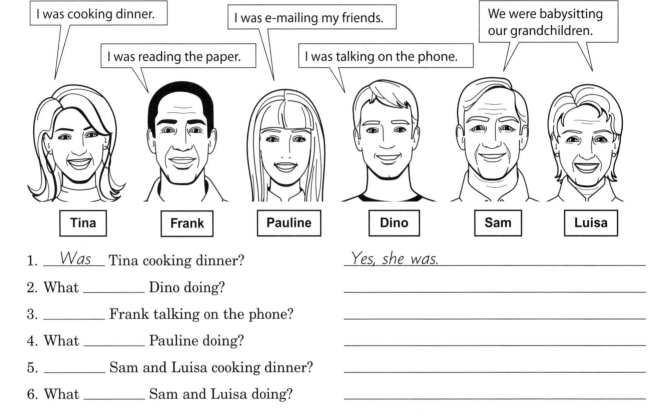

> I was cooking dinner.
>
> I was reading the paper.
>
> I was e-mailing my friends.
>
> I was talking on the phone.
>
> We were babysitting our grandchildren.

Tina   **Frank**   **Pauline**   **Dino**   **Sam**   **Luisa**

1. ___Was___ Tina cooking dinner?   _Yes, she was._ _____

2. What _____ Dino doing?   _____

3. _____ Frank talking on the phone?   _____

4. What _____ Pauline doing?   _____

5. _____ Sam and Luisa cooking dinner? _____

6. What _____ Sam and Luisa doing?   _____

B Correct the mistakes. There are two mistakes in each sentence.

1. What Beth was do‸ yesterday morning? *ing*

2. Teresa and Jimmy was watch TV all day.

3. I was talk my friend on Monday night.

4. Were he writting a letter?

5. What was you wear yesterday?

6. I were baking cake for my daughter.

C What were you and your family doing at each of these times yesterday?

Example: 7:00 a.m. _I was sleeping. My children were watching TV._

7:00 a.m.	
9:00 a.m.	
noon	
3:00 p.m.	
6:00 p.m.	
10:00 p.m.	

Lesson C Past continuous and simple past

A Complete the sentences with the past continuous or the simple past.

1. Julia __*was working*__ in the garden when she saw the fire.
   (work)

2. I was driving too fast around a corner when I _____
   (hit)
   a tree.

3. While Frank _____ dinner, his sister called.
   (cook)

4. The fire alarm went off while we _____ a break.
   (take)

5. When the burglar _____ into the house, they were visiting
   (break)
   the neighbors.

6. When the rain started, we _____ in the library.
   (study)

B Rewrite the sentences.

1. While Bill was eating dinner, he heard a noise in the garden.

   Bill __*heard a noise in the garden*__ while __*he was eating dinner*__ .

2. While Bohai and Sofia were waiting for a bus, they phoned their friends.

   Bohai and Sofia phoned _____ while _____ .

3. When Liana and I heard the fire alarm, we were taking a test.

   Liana and I were _____ when _____ .

4. Teresa was eating a sandwich when she broke her tooth.

   When Teresa _____, she _____ .

5. When Mr. and Mrs. Ramirez came home, they were carrying a lot of bags.

   Mr. and Mrs. Ramirez were _____ when _____ .

6. Joe and Omar saw a deer while they were jogging in the park.

   While Joe and Omar were _____, they _____ .

C Answer the question about you.

What were you carrying when you arrived at your English class today?

_____

Lesson C Past continuous and simple past

A Complete the sentences with the past continuous or the simple past.

1. (work / see) Julia ____was working____ in the garden when she
   _____saw_____ the fire.

2. (drive / hit) I _____ too fast around a corner when I
   _____ a tree.

3. (cook / call) While Frank _____ dinner, his sister
   _____ .

4. (go / take) The fire alarm _____ off while we
   _____ a break.

5. (break / visit) When the burglar _____ into the house, they
   _____ the neighbors.

6. (start / study) When the rain _____ , we
   _____ in the library.

B Rewrite the sentences.

1. While Bill was eating dinner, he heard a noise in the garden.
   Bill _heard a noise in the garden_ while _he was eating dinner_ .

2. While Bohai and Sofia were waiting for a bus, they phoned their friends.
   Bohai and Sophia _____ while _____ .

3. When Liana and I heard the fire alarm, we were taking a test.
   Liana and I _____ when _____ .

4. Teresa was eating a sandwich when she broke her tooth.
   When _____ , she _____ .

5. When Mr. and Mrs. Ramirez came home, they were carrying a lot of bags.
   Mr. and Mrs. Ramirez _____ when _____ .

6. Joe and Omar saw a deer while they were jogging in the park.
   While _____ , they _____ .

C Answer the questions about you.

1. What were you carrying when you arrived at your English class today?
   _____

2. Where did you stop while you were coming to class today?
   _____

Lesson C *Past continuous and simple past*

A Complete the sentences with the past continuous or simple past of the correct verb.

break	cook	go	see	study	visit
call	drive	hit	start	take	work

1. Julia __was working__ in the garden when she _____saw_____ the fire.

2. I _____ too fast around a corner when I _____ a tree.

3. While Frank _____ dinner, his sister _____ .

4. The fire alarm _____ off while we _____ a break.

5. When the burglar _____ into the house, they _____ the neighbors.

6. When the rain _____ , we _____ in the library.

B Rewrite the sentences.

1. While Bill was eating dinner, he heard a noise in the garden.

   Bill _heard a noise in the garden while he was eating dinner_ .

2. While Bohai and Sofia were waiting for a bus, they phoned their friends.

   Bohai and Sofia _____ .

3. When Liana and I heard the fire alarm, we were taking a test.

   Liana and I _____ .

4. Teresa was eating a sandwich when she broke her tooth.

   When _____ .

5. When Mr. and Mrs. Ramirez came home, they were carrying a lot of bags.

   Mr. and Mrs. Ramirez _____ .

6. Joe and Omar saw a deer while they were jogging in the park.

   While _____ .

C Answer the questions about you.

1. What were you carrying when you arrived at your English class today?

   _____

2. Where did you stop while you were coming to class today?

   _____

3. What were you doing when your teacher started English class today?

   _____

Lesson D *Reading*

☑ ■ ■

A Match the words with the definitions.

1. gathering *b*   a. people you don't know

2. to evacuate _____   b. collecting

3. generous _____   c. completely damaged

4. strangers _____   d. to leave a dangerous place

5. destroyed _____   e. took quickly

6. grabbed _____   f. helpful and giving

B Read the article. Complete the text. Use the words from Exercise A.

A Difficult Time

About two years ago, there was a big fire upstairs in our apartment building. We heard the fire alarm while we were eating our dinner. Then we heard fire engines on the street. While my husband was __*gathering*__ our important documents, I
1

_____ some clothes and put them into a suitcase. A few minutes later, we
2

ran downstairs. Smoke was coming out of the windows on the fifth floor. The police ordered everyone to _____ .
3

While we were standing outside, some _____ asked us if we needed help.
4

They invited us to stay at their home. They were so _____ . We thanked
5

them but decided to stay at my parents' house. The fire _____ our building.
6

Luckily, we had fire insurance. One year later, we moved into a new apartment. I'll never forget those kind strangers who offered to help us at a very difficult time.

C Number the events from the story in the correct sequence.

_____ We evacuated our apartment.   _____ We grabbed our documents and some clothes.

_____ Some strangers talked to us.   _____ The fire engines arrived.

_1_ We heard a fire alarm.   _____ We ran downstairs.

D Describe a time when you received help from a friend, a neighbor, or a stranger. Write a few sentences. Use the back of this paper.

Lesson D Reading

A Complete the words to match the definitions.

1. g _a_ _t_ _h_ _e_ _r_ _i_ _n_ _g_ : collecting

2. to e ___ ___ ___ ___ ___ ___ ___ : to leave a dangerous place

3. g ___ ___ ___ ___ ___ ___ ___ : helpful and giving

4. s ___ ___ ___ ___ ___ ___ ___ ___ : people you don't know

5. d ___ ___ ___ ___ ___ ___ ___ ___ : completely damaged

6. g ___ ___ ___ ___ ___ ___ : took quickly

B Read the article. Complete the text. Use the words from Exercise A.

A Difficult Time

About two years ago, there was a big fire upstairs in our apartment building. We heard the fire alarm while we were eating our dinner. Then we heard the fire engines on the street. While my husband was __gathering__ our important documents, I
                                                        1
_____ some clothes and put them into a suitcase. A few minutes later, we
            2
ran downstairs. Smoke was coming out of the windows on the fifth floor. The police ordered everyone to _____ .
                                    3

While we were standing outside, some _____ asked us if we needed help.
                                                    4
They invited us to stay at their home. They were so _____ . We thanked
                                                            5
them but decided to stay at my parents' house. The fire _____ our building.
                                                                6
Luckily, we had fire insurance. One year later, we moved into a new apartment. I'll never forget those kind strangers who offered to help us at a very difficult time.

C Number the events from the story in the correct sequence.

_____ We evacuated our apartment.   _____ The fire engines arrived.

_____ Some strangers talked to us.   _____ We ran downstairs.

_1_ We heard a fire alarm.   _____ We stayed with my parents.

_____ We grabbed our documents and some clothes.   _____ We moved into a new apartment.

D Describe a time when you received help from a friend, a neighbor, or a stranger. Write several sentences. Use the back of this paper.

A Write the words for the definitions.

1. g*athering* _____: collecting
2. e_____: to leave a dangerous place
3. g_____: helpful and giving
4. s_____: people you don't know
5. d_____: completely damaged
6. g_____: took quickly

B Read the article. Complete the text. Use the words from Exercise A.

A Difficult Time

About two years ago, there was a big fire upstairs in our apartment building. We heard the fire alarm while we were eating our dinner. Then we heard the fire engines on the street. While my husband was ___*gathering*___ our important documents, I
_____ some clothes and put them into a suitcase. A few minutes later, we
            2
ran downstairs. Smoke was coming out of the windows on the fifth floor. The police ordered everyone to _____ .
                              3

While we were standing outside, some _____ asked us if we needed help.
                                                    4
They invited us to stay at their home. They were so _____ . We thanked
                                                              5
them but decided to stay at my parents' house. The fire _____ our building.
                                                                    6
Luckily, we had fire insurance. One year later, we moved into a new apartment. I'll never forget those kind strangers who offered to help us at a very difficult time.

C Number the events from the story in the correct sequence.

_____ We evacuated our apartment.   _____ The fire engines arrived.

_____ Some strangers talked to us.   _____ We ran downstairs.

__1__ We heard a fire alarm.   _____ We stayed with my parents.

_____ We grabbed our documents and some clothes. _____ We moved into a new apartment.

D Describe a time when you received help from a friend, a neighbor, or a stranger. Write a paragraph. Use the back of this paper.

Lesson **E** *Writing*

A Read the story. Complete the questions. Use *what*, *where*, *when*, *why*, or *how*.

Rabbit Rescue

Two days ago, I was walking near the lake when I saw a woman with a big dog. The dog was chasing after a rabbit. The rabbit was scared and jumped into the lake. Then the dog jumped into the lake and swam after the rabbit. The dog's owner was very worried and started to call the dog. I stood with her by the side of the lake to see what would happen. When the rabbit got to the middle of the lake, it started to feel tired. By then the dog was near the rabbit. So the rabbit jumped on the dog's back, and the dog swam back with the rabbit on its back. They both got back safely, very wet and tired.

1. __*What*__ is the story about?   The story is about a woman, a rabbit, and a dog.

2. _____ did the story happen?   Two days ago.

3. _____ did it happen?   Near the lake.

4. _____ was the woman doing?   She was walking her dog.

5. _____ happened?   The dog chased a rabbit into the lake.

6. _____ was the woman worried?   Because her dog was swimming in the lake.

7. _____ did the story end?   The dog saved the rabbit.

B Think of a time when you were worried or scared. What happened? Write three sentences.

_____

_____

_____

A Read the story. Answer the questions.

Rabbit Rescue

Two days ago, I was walking near the lake when I saw a woman with a big dog. The dog was chasing after a rabbit. The rabbit was scared and jumped into the lake. Then the dog jumped into the lake and swam after the rabbit. The dog's owner was very worried and started to call the dog. I stood with her by the side of the lake to see what would happen. When the rabbit got to the middle of the lake, it started to feel tired. By then the dog was near the rabbit. So the rabbit jumped on the dog's back, and the dog swam back with the rabbit on its back. They both got back safely, very wet and tired.

1. What is the story about?   *The story is about a woman, a rabbit, and a dog.*

2. When did the story happen?   _____

3. Where did it happen?   _____

4. What was the woman doing?   _____

5. What happened?   _____

6. Why was the woman worried?   _____

7. How did the story end?   _____

B Think of a time when you were worried or scared. What happened? Write several sentences.

_____

_____

_____

_____

_____

A Read the story. Write questions. Use *what*, *where*, *when*, *why*, or *how*.

Rabbit Rescue

Two days ago, I was walking near the lake when I saw a woman with a big dog. The dog was chasing after a rabbit. The rabbit was scared and jumped into the lake. Then the dog jumped into the lake and swam after the rabbit. The dog's owner was very worried and started to call the dog. I stood with her by the side of the lake to see what would happen. When the rabbit got to the middle of the lake, it started to feel tired. By then the dog was near the rabbit. So the rabbit jumped on the dog's back, and the dog swam back with the rabbit on its back. They both got back safely, very wet and tired.

1. *What is the story about?*   The story is about a woman, a rabbit, and a dog.

2. _____ Two days ago.

3. _____ Near the lake.

4. _____ She was walking her dog.

5. _____ The dog chased a rabbit into the lake.

6. _____ Because her dog was swimming in the lake.

7. _____ The dog saved the rabbit.

B Think of a time when you were worried or scared. What happened? Write a paragraph. Use the back of this paper if necessary.

_____

_____

_____

_____

_____

A Look at the chart. Circle *True* or *False*.

What makes your neighborhood safe?		
1 2 3 4 5		
most important least important		
	The Gomez family	The Park family
Helpful neighbors	2	1
Neighborhood watch	5	3
Police officers	3	2
Home security alarms	4	4
Good street lighting	1	5

1. The Gomez family thinks that good street lighting is the most important. (True) False

2. The Park family thinks that security alarms are the most important. True False

3. Helpful neighbors are more important for the Park family than for the Gomez family. True False

4. Police officers are more important for the Gomez family than for the Park family. True False

5. Neighborhood watch has the same importance for both families. True False

B Why do you need these things in your home or school? Match.

1. You need an emergency exit map _d_   a. to see the exits clearly.

2. You need a fire extinguisher ____   b. to warn everyone to evacuate.

3. You need a fire alarm ____   c. to put out a fire.

4. You need a first-aid kit ____   d. to find the exit.

5. You need emergency exit signs ____   e. to help someone with an injury.

C Internet task: Find ways of preventing fires or accidents in your home. Write one piece of advice. If you don't have access to the Internet, use your experience to give advice.

Advice: _____

Lesson F Another view

A Look at the chart. Circle the correct answers.

What makes your neighborhood safe?					
1	2	3	4	5	
most important				least important	

	The Gomez family	The Park family
Helpful neighbors	2	1
Neighborhood watch	5	3
Police officers	3	2
Home security alarms	4	4
Good street lighting	1	5

1. What is most important for the Gomez family?
   a. neighborhood watch   b. police officers   (c.) good street lighting

2. What is most important for the Park family?
   a. helpful neighbors   b. neighborhood watch   c. home security alarms

3. What is more important for the Park family than for the Gomez family?
   a. home security alarms   b. helpful neighbors   c. good street lighting

4. What is more important for the Gomez family than for the Park family?
   a. helpful neighbors   b. police officers   c. good street lighting

5. What has the same importance for both families?
   a. neighborhood watch   b. good street lighting   c. home security alarms

B Why do you need these things in your home or school? Complete the sentences.

find   help   put out   see   warn

1. You need an emergency exit map to _____*find*_____ the exit.

2. You need a fire extinguisher to _____ a fire.

3. You need a fire alarm to _____ everyone to evacuate.

4. You need a first-aid kit to _____ someone with an injury.

5. You need emergency exit signs to _____ the exits clearly.

C Internet task: Find ways of preventing fires or accidents in your home. Write two pieces of advice. Use the back of this paper. If you don't have access to the Internet, use your experience to give advice.

Lesson **F** *Another view*

A Look at the chart. Answer the questions.

What makes your neighborhood safe?		
1 2 3 4 5		
most important		least important
	The Gomez family	The Park family
Helpful neighbors	2	1
Neighborhood watch	5	3
Police officers	3	2
Home security alarms	4	4
Good street lighting	1	5

1. What is most important for the Gomez family? *Good street lighting.*

2. What is most important for the Park family? _____

3. What is more important for the Park family than for the Gomez family?

    _____

4. What is more important for the Gomez family than for the Park family?

    _____

5. What has the same importance for both families? _____

B Why do you need these things in your home or school? Write reasons.

1. You need an emergency exit map to *find the exit* _____ .

2. You need a fire extinguisher to _____ .

3. You need a fire alarm to _____ .

4. You need a first-aid kit to _____ .

5. You need emergency exit signs to _____ .

C Internet task: Find ways of preventing fires or accidents in your home.
Write three pieces of advice. If you don't have access to the Internet, use
your experience to give advice.

Advice: _____

_____

_____

Lesson A *Get ready*

A Complete the conversation.

days off	discount	in advance	reserve	round-trip	tax

Jenny I want to ask my boss for a few ___*days off*___ next week. I really need a vacation.

Ramona That's a good idea! Where do you want to go?

Jenny I want to go to New York, but I don't have enough money to fly.

Ramona If you book a flight _____ , you can get a _____ .

Jenny I know, but the hotels are very expensive, too.

Ramona That's true. With room _____ , it can be over $200 a night. Why don't you go somewhere cheaper?

Jenny That's a good idea. I could go camping instead. I'd like to go to the beach.

A _____ ticket by bus is only $60.

Ramona You'll need to _____ a campsite before you go. But it will be much cheaper than New York.

Jenny And more relaxing, too!

B Solve the problem.

Hannah and Mark have $800 to spend on their vacation. They want to go to Miami for three nights. Each round-trip flight will cost $200. The hotel will cost $95 per night plus $12 room tax per night. How much money will they have left?

Round-trip ticket × 2   _____

Hotel for three nights   _____

Room tax for three nights   _____

Total   _____

Amount left   _____

C Where did you go for your last trip or vacation? How much did you spend on transportation and lodging?

Vacation/trip to _____

Transportation by _____ = $ _____

Lodging: $ _____ × _____ nights = $ _____

Room tax: $ _____ × _____ nights = ___$ _____

                        Total: $ _____

Lesson A *Get ready*

A Complete the conversation.

cheaper	discount	in advance	round-trip	vacation
days off	expensive	reserve	tax	

Jenny I want to ask my boss for a few ___*days off*___ next week. I

really need a _____ .

Ramona That's a good idea! Where do you want to go?

Jenny I want to go to New York, but I don't have enough money to fly.

Ramona If you book a flight _____ , you can get a

_____ .

Jenny I know, but the hotels are very _____ , too.

Ramona That's true. With room _____ , it can be over $200 a
night. Why don't you go somewhere cheaper?

Jenny That's a good idea. I could go camping instead. I'd like to go to

the beach. A _____ ticket by bus is only $60.

Ramona You'll need to _____ a campsite before you go. But it will

be much _____ than New York.

Jenny And more relaxing, too!

B Solve the problems.

1. Hannah and Mark have $800 to spend on their vacation. They want to
go to Miami for three nights. Each round-trip flight will cost $200. The
hotel will cost $95 per night plus $12 room tax per night. How much
money will they have left?

   _____

2. Katerina has $600 to spend on a vacation. She wants to go to
Philadelphia for two nights. The flight will cost $300. The hotel will cost
$115 per night plus $16 room tax per night. She can get a $20 discount
per night if she books online. How much money will she have left?

   _____

C Where did you go for your last trip or vacation? How much did you spend
on transportation, lodging, and food? Write a budget for your trip. Use the
back of this paper.

A Complete the conversation. Put the conversation in the correct order.

days off	discount	in advance	reserve	round-trip	tax

_1_   **Jenny** I want to ask my boss for a few __days off__ next week. I really need a vacation.

____ **Ramona** That's true. With room _____ , it can be over $200 a night. Why don't you go somewhere cheaper?

____ **Ramona** If you book a flight _____ , you can get a

_____ .

____ **Jenny** I know, but the hotels are very expensive, too.

____ **Ramona** You'll need to _____ a campsite before you go. But it will be much cheaper than New York.

____ **Ramona** That's a good idea! Where do you want to go?

____ **Jenny** That's a good idea. I could go camping instead. I'd like to go

to the beach. A _____ ticket by bus is only $60.

____ **Jenny** I want to go to New York, but I don't have enough money to fly.

____ **Jenny** And more relaxing, too!

B Solve the problems. Write one more problem. Use the back of this paper.

1. Hannah and Mark have $800 to spend on their vacation. They want to go to Miami for three nights. Each round-trip flight will cost $200. The hotel will cost $95 per night plus $12 room tax per night. How much money will they have left?

_____

2. Katerina has $600 to spend on a vacation. She wants to go to Philadelphia for two nights. The flight will cost $300. The hotel will cost $115 per night plus $16 room tax per night. She can get a $20 discount per night if she books online. How much money will she have left?

_____

C Where did you go for your last trip or vacation? How much did you spend on transportation and lodging? How much did you spend on food and entertainment? What other expenses did you have? Write a budget for your trip. Use the back of this paper.

Lesson B *Dependent clauses*

Name: _____

A Match.

1. If I find a cheap air ticket, __f__   a. if there is enough snow.

2. What will you do ____   b. they'll go camping.

3. We won't go to the concert ____   c. if you get a few days off?

4. They will go skiing ____   d. she'll visit a museum.

5. If they don't find a hotel, ____   e. if the tickets are too expensive.

6. If Rita has enough time, ____   f. I'll fly to Costa Rica.

B Write questions. Use the simple present or future form of the verbs.

1. (Pete / do / save)

   What *will Pete do* _____ if he _____ *saves* _____ some money?

2. (Janine / buy / go)

   What _____ if she _____ to the mall?

3. (Ron / go / get)

   Where _____ if he _____ a vacation?

4. (Carlos / do / not go)

   What _____ if he _____ to the movies?

5. (Anna and her family / go / not rain)

   Where _____ if it _____ on Saturday?

6. (Len and Flora / wear / go)

   What _____ if they _____ to the party?

C Correct the mistakes. Add the missing word.

1. If we have a few days off, we ^*will* go camping.   (will)

2. If snows, we'll take our snow boots.   (it)

3. They take a vacation if prices are not too high.   (will)

4. I won't go swimming it rains.   (if)

5. Julio won't go to the party if starts too late.   (it)

6. Barbara will take the children to the zoo if has time.   (she)

Lesson B *Dependent clauses*

A Complete the sentences with the simple present or future form of the verbs.

1. (find / fly) If I ___*find*___ a cheap air ticket, I'*ll fly*____ to Costa Rica.

2. (do / get) What _____ you _____ if you _____ a few days off?

3. (not go / be) We _____ to the concert if the tickets _____ too expensive.

4. (go / be) They _____ skiing if there _____ enough snow.

5. (not find / go) If they _____ a hotel, they _____ camping.

6. (have / visit) If Rita _____ enough time, she _____ a museum.

B Write questions. Use *if.*

1. (Pete / do / save some money)

   What will _Pete do if he saves some money_____ ?

2. (Janine / buy / go to the mall)

   What will _____ ?

3. (Ron / go / get a vacation)

   Where will _____ ?

4. (Carlos / do / not go to the movies)

   What will _____ ?

5. (Anna and her family / go / not rain on Saturday)

   Where will _____ ?

6. (Len and Flora / wear / go to the party)

   What will _____ ?

C Correct the mistakes. Add the missing word.

| if | it | it | she | will | will |

1. If we have a few days off, we ^*will* go camping.

2. If snows, we'll take our snow boots.

3. They take a vacation if prices are not too high.

4. I won't go swimming it rains.

5. Julio won't go to the party if starts too late.

6. Barbara will take the children to the zoo if has time.

Lesson B *Dependent clauses*

■■☑

A Complete the sentences.

1. If I find a cheap air ticket, _____*I'll fly to Costa Rica*_____ .
   (fly / Costa Rica)

2. What will you do if _____ ?
   (get / a few days off)

3. We won't go to the concert if _____ .
   (tickets / too expensive)

4. They will go skiing if _____ .
   (enough snow)

5. If they don't find a hotel, _____ .
   (go camping)

6. If Rita has enough time, _____ .
   (visit a museum)

B Write questions. Use *if.* Use the present simple or future form of the verbs.

1. (What / Pete / do / save some money)
   What will Pete do if he saves some money?

2. (What / Janine / buy / go to the mall)
   _____

3. (Where / Ron / go / get a vacation)
   _____

4. (What / Carlos / do / not go to the movies)
   _____

5. (Where / Anna and her family / go / not rain on Saturday)
   _____

6. (What / Len and Flora / wear / go to the party)
   _____

C Correct the mistakes. Add the missing word.

1. If we have a few days off, we ᴧgo camping.
                                 will

2. If snows, we'll take our snow boots.

3. They take a vacation if prices are not too high.

4. I won't go swimming it rains.

5. Julio won't go to the party if starts too late.

6. Barbara will take the children to the zoo if has time.

A Complete the sentences with the simple present or future form of the verbs.

1. (travel / study) Before I ____travel____ to Italy, I'll _study_ Italian.

2. (go / buy) Before Vera _____ camping, she _____ a tent.

3. (arrive / call) After Angela _____ at the airport, she
_____ her parents.

4. (make / collect) Pablo and Jun _____ a fire after they
_____ some wood.

5. (get / fly) Wanda _____ a new cell phone before she
_____ to Europe.

6. (eat / pay) After we _____ breakfast, we _____ our
hotel bill.

B Rewrite the sentences. Use *before* or *after*.

1. Before I go to Paris, I'll learn French.
After I _learn French, I'll go to Paris_____ .

2. Luis and Paolo will buy a street map after they check into their hotel.
Luis and Paolo _____ before _____ .

3. Before Aleesha goes on vacation, she will visit her cousins in Florida.
After Aleesha _____ , _____ .

4. We will take the city tour before we have lunch.
We _____ after _____ .

5. After Sam and Cindy eat dinner, they will go to a dance club.
Before Sam and Cindy _____ , _____ .

6. Omar will finish packing his suitcase before he watches a movie.
Omar _____ after _____ .

C Answer the question about yourself.

What will you do before you go on your next vacation?

_____

Lesson C *Dependent clauses*

A Complete the sentences with the simple present or future form of the verbs.

arrive	call	eat	get	make	study
buy	collect	fly	go	pay	travel

1. Before I ___*travel*___ to Italy, I'*ll study*_____ Italian.

2. Before Vera _____ camping, she _____ a tent.

3. After Angela _____ at the airport, she _____ her parents.

4. Pablo and Jun _____ a fire after they _____ some wood.

5. Wanda _____ a new cell phone before she _____ to Europe.

6. After we _____ breakfast, we _____ our hotel bill.

B Rewrite the sentences. Use *before* or *after*.

1. Before I go to Paris, I'll learn French.

   After I *learn French, I'll go to Paris*_____ .

2. Luis and Paolo will buy a street map after they check into their hotel.

   Luis and Pablo _____ .

3. Before Aleesha goes on vacation, she will visit her cousins in Florida.

   After Aleesha _____ .

4. We will take the city tour before we have lunch.

   We _____ .

5. After Sam and Cindy eat dinner, they will go to a dance club.

   Before Sam and Cindy _____ .

6. Omar will finish packing his suitcase before he watches a movie.

   Omar _____ .

C Answer the questions about yourself.

1. What will you do before you go on your next vacation?

   _____

2. What will you do after you finish school today?

   _____

Lesson C *Dependent clauses*

A Complete the sentences with the simple present or future form of an appropriate verb.

1. Before I ___*travel*___ to Italy, I'll ___*study*___ Italian.

2. Before Vera _____ camping, she _____ a tent.

3. After Angela _____ at the airport, she _____ her parents.

4. Pablo and Jun _____ a fire after they _____ some wood.

5. Wanda _____ a new cell phone before she _____ to Europe.

6. After we _____ breakfast, we _____ our hotel bill.

B Rewrite the sentences. Use *before* or *after*.

1. Before I go to Paris, I'll learn French. (After)

   After I learn French, I'll go to Paris.

2. Luis and Paolo will buy a street map after they check into their hotel. (before)

   _____

3. Before Aleesha goes on vacation, she will visit her cousins in Florida. (After)

   _____

4. We will take the city tour before we have lunch. (after)

   _____

5. After Sam and Cindy eat dinner, they will go to a dance club. (Before)

   _____

6. Omar will finish packing his suitcase before he watches a movie. (after)

   _____

C Answer the questions about yourself.

1. What will you do before you go on your next vacation?

   _____

2. What will you do after you finish school today?

   _____

3. What will you do before you go to bed tonight?

   _____

Lesson D Reading

A Match the words with the definitions.

1. attraction __c__   a. to get away

2. admission ____   b. to finish the supply of tickets

3. in advance ____   c. a place that tourists like to visit

4. to sell out ____   d. special boats to carry people and cars

5. to escape ____   e. the cost of a ticket

6. ferries ____   f. before

B Read the article. Complete the text. Use the words from Exercise A.

Martha's Vineyard

A popular tourist destination in New England is Martha's Vineyard, an island off the eastern coast of the United States. It is especially popular with people from Boston or New York who want to ___*escape*___ the hot summers.
                                                    1

To get to Martha's Vineyard, you go to Hyannis and get on one of the _____ to
                                                                                                2
the island. In the summer, it is wise to book your tickets _____ because the boats
                                                                                    3
are very crowded and they _____ early in the day.
                                            4

The main _____ on Martha's Vineyard is the beaches. The water is cool and
                        5
very clean. It is a good place for swimming, cycling, walking, and bird watching. You can
also visit the Martha's Vineyard Museum. The _____ is $7 for adults, $4 for
                                                            6
children.

C Circle the correct answers.

1. What is Martha's Vineyard?
   a. a town
   b. an island
   c. a beach

2. Why do tourists like to go there?
   a. It's cool.
   b. It's empty.
   c. It's crowded.

3. What do you need to buy in advance?
   a. museum tickets
   b. bus tickets
   c. ferry tickets

4. Which activity is popular there?
   a. climbing
   b. cycling
   c. camping

Lesson D Reading

■ ☑ ■

A Complete the words to match the definitions.

1. a _t_ _t_ _r_ _a_ _c_ _t_ _i_ _o_ _n_ : a place that tourists like to visit

2. a __ __ __ __ __ __ __ __ : the cost of a ticket

3. i __ __ __ __ __ __ __ __ : before

4. to s __ __ __ __ __ __ : to finish the supply of tickets

5. to e __ __ __ __ __ : to get away

6. f __ __ __ __ __ __ : special boats to carry people and cars

B Read the article. Complete the text. Use the words from Exercise A.

Martha's Vineyard

A popular tourist destination in New England is Martha's Vineyard, an island off the eastern coast of the United States. It is especially popular with people from Boston or New York who want to ___escape___ the hot summers.
₁

To get to Martha's Vineyard, you go to Hyannis and get on one of the _____ to
₂
the island. In the summer, it is wise to book your tickets _____ because the boats
₃
are very crowded and they _____ early in the day.
₄

The main _____ on Martha's Vineyard is the beaches. The water is cool and
₅
very clean. It is a good place for swimming, cycling, walking, and bird watching. You can
also visit the Martha's Vineyard Museum. The _____ is $7 for adults, $4 for
₆
children.

C Circle the correct answers.

1. What is Martha's Vineyard?
   a. a town   c. a beach
   (b.) an island   d. a museum

2. Why do tourists like to go there?
   a. It's cool.   c. It's crowded.
   b. It's empty.   d. It's far away.

3. What do you need to buy in advance?
   a. museum tickets   c. ferry tickets
   b. bus tickets   d. parking tickets

4. Which activity is popular there?
   a. climbing   c. camping
   b. cycling   d. shopping

Lesson D Reading

A Write the words to match the definitions.

1. a_<u>ttraction</u>_____: a place that tourists like to visit

2. a_____: the cost of a ticket

3. in a_____: before

4. to s_____ o_____: to finish the supply of tickets

5. to e_____: to get away

6. f_____: special boats to carry people and cars

B Read the article. Complete the text. Use the words from Exercise A.

Martha's Vineyard

A popular tourist destination in New England is Martha's Vineyard, an island off the eastern coast of the United States. It is especially popular with people from Boston or New York who want to ___<u>escape</u>___ the hot summers.
                              1

To get to Martha's Vineyard, you go to Hyannis and get on one of the _____ to
                                                                              2
the island. In the summer, it is wise to book your tickets _____ because the boats
                                                              3
are very crowded and they _____ early in the day.
                              4

The main _____ on Martha's Vineyard is the beaches. The water is cool and
             5
very clean. It is a good place for swimming, cycling, walking, and bird watching. You can
also visit the Martha's Vineyard Museum. The _____ is $7 for adults, $4 for
                                                   6
children.

C Answer the questions.

1. What is Martha's Vineyard?

   _____<u>An island.</u>_____

2. Why do tourists like to go there?

   _____

3. What do you need to buy in advance?

   _____

4. Which activities are popular there?

   _____

Lesson E *Writing*

A Read the paragraph.

Lincoln Park Zoo

One of the most popular zoos in the Midwest is Lincoln Park Zoo in Chicago, Illinois. It is located on North Clark Street near the center of the city. It is open from 10:00 a.m. to 7:00 p.m. every day except Mondays. Admission is free. The zoo has something for everyone. It has animals from all over the world. If you like elephants and tigers, you can go on the African safari ride. If you like birds, you will enjoy the scenic paddleboat cruise. If you have children, they will love the Story Time entertainment. If you want to relax, you can go to the Big Cats Café and enjoy ice cream. At the end of your visit, you can buy gifts in the zoo store. Children and adults love to visit Lincoln Park Zoo.

B Answer the questions.

1. What is the main topic of the paragraph?

   Things you can do at Lincoln Park Zoo

2. Which are examples of things to do at the zoo? Check (✓) four things.

   ☐ It is in Chicago.
   ☐ It is not open on Mondays.
   ☐ Admission is free.
   ☐ You can see elephants and tigers.
   ☐ It has animals from all over the world.

   ☐ You can go on an African safari.
   ☐ You can take children.
   ☐ You can go on a cruise.
   ☐ You can eat ice cream.

3. What can you do at the end of your visit?

   _____

C What tourist attraction have you visited? Write the information.

Name of attraction: _____

Where is it located? _____

How much is the admission? _____

What can you do there?

1. _____

2. _____

Name: _____

Lesson E **Writing**

A Complete the paragraph.

If you like elephants and tigers	If you have children
If you want to relax	If you like birds

Lincoln Park Zoo

One of the most popular zoos in the Midwest is Lincoln Park
Zoo in Chicago, Illinois. It is located on North Clark Street near
the center of the city. It is open from 10:00 a.m. to 7:00 p.m. every
day except Mondays. Admission is free. The zoo has something
for everyone. It has animals from all over the world.
If you like elephants and tigers , you can go on the African
safari ride. _____ , you will enjoy the scenic
paddleboat cruise. _____ , they will love
the Story Time entertainment. _____ , you can go to the Big Cats Café
and enjoy ice cream. At the end of your visit, you can buy gifts in the zoo store. Children and
adults love to visit Lincoln Park Zoo.

B Answer the questions.

1. What is the main topic of the paragraph?

   Things you can do at Lincoln Park Zoo

2. What are four things to do at the zoo?

   a. _____   c. _____

   b. _____   d. _____

3. What can you do at the end of your visit?

   _____

C What tourist attraction have you visited recently? Write the information. Use
dependent clauses with *If*.

Name of attraction: _____

Where is it located? _____

How much is the admission? _____

What can you do there?

1. If _____ .

2. If _____ .

Lesson **E** *Writing*

A Complete the paragraph.

If you like elephants and tigers	At the end of your visit	If you have children
Admission is free.	If you want to relax	If you like birds

Lincoln Park Zoo

One of the most popular zoos in the Midwest is Lincoln Park Zoo in Chicago, Illinois. It is located on North Clark Street near the center of the city. It is open from 10:00 a.m. to 7:00 p.m. every day except Mondays. *Admission is free.* The zoo has something for everyone. It has animals from all over the world. _____ , you can go on the African safari ride. _____ , you will enjoy the scenic paddleboat cruise. _____ , they will love the Story Time entertainment. _____ , you can go to the Big Cats Café and enjoy ice cream. _____ , you can buy gifts in the zoo store. Children and adults love to visit Lincoln Park Zoo.

B Answer the questions.

1. What is the main topic of the paragraph?

   Things you can do at Lincoln Park Zoo

2. What are five things to do at the zoo?

   a. _____   d. _____

   b. _____   e. _____

   c. _____

3. What can you do at the end of your visit?

   _____

C What tourist attraction have you visited? Complete the chart. Then write a paragraph on the back of this paper. Use dependent clauses with *If*.

Name of attraction	
Location	
Admission	
What can you do there?	

Name: _____

Lesson F *Another view*

A Read the clues. Complete the crossword puzzle.

Clues

Across

1. You should do this before you go to a campsite or a hotel.

3. You can stay here when you go on vacation.

5. A place that tourists like to visit

6. The cost of entry to a museum

Down

2. Everyone needs this to have time to relax.

4. A person who likes to travel and go sightseeing

B Imagine you are going to do the activities below. Write four sentences. Use *before* or *after*. Write on the back of this paper.

Example: *Before I go camping, I'll reserve a campsite.*

go camping

go shopping   go skiing

go running

Name:

Lesson F *Another view*

A Read the clues. Complete the crossword puzzle.

Clues

Across

1. You should do this before you go to a campsite or a hotel.
3. You can stay here when you go on vacation.
5. A place that tourists like to visit
6. The cost of entry to a museum

Down

2. Everyone needs this to have time to relax.
4. A person who likes to travel and go sightseeing

B Imagine you are going to do the activities below. Write two sentences for each picture. Use *before* or *after*. Write on the back of this paper.

Example: *Before I go camping, I'll reserve a campsite.*

go camping

go shopping

go skiing

go running

A Read the clues. Guess the words. Then number the clues and complete the crossword puzzle.

Clues

___1___ You should do this before you go to a campsite or a hotel. _____*reserve*_____

_____ The cost of entry to a museum _____

_____ Everyone needs this to have time to relax. _____

_____ A place that tourists like to visit _____

_____ A person who likes to travel and go sightseeing _____

_____ You can stay here when you go on vacation. _____

B Imagine you are going to do the activities below. Write four sentences for each picture. Use *before* and *after*. Write on the back of this paper.

Example: _Before I go camping, I'll reserve a campsite._

go camping

go shopping

go skiing

go running

Answer key

Unit 1: Personal information

Lesson A: Get ready pages 1–3

A

Paulo stayed home and watched TV. There was a movie on Saturday afternoon. He ate popcorn. Then he read a book and went to bed early. He was alone all day.

Andrea met some friends in a café. They drank coffee and talked. Then she went to a dance club with her friends. They danced until 1:00 a.m.

B

1. Paolo is shy.
2. Paolo isn't outgoing.
3. Paolo likes reading.
4. Andrea is friendly.
5. Andrea isn't quiet.
6. Andrea dislikes being alone.

C

Answers will vary.

Lesson B: Verbs + gerunds
pages 4–6

A

Drop 'e': dancing, taking, writing
Double consonant: getting, shopping, swimming
No change: doing, eating, staying

B

1. Nina likes listening to music.
2. Erin enjoys doing homework.
3. Ahmad likes watching movies.
4. Yolanda and Sam hate paying bills.
5. Trudy dislikes taking out the garbage.
6. Alma and Lara don't mind cleaning the house.

C

1. Does Nina like swimming? Yes, she does.
2. Does Ahmad love dancing? Yes, he does.
3. Do Yolanda and Sam hate shopping? Yes, they do.
4. Does Trudy mind cleaning? No, she doesn't.

5. Do Alma and Lara dislike playing cards? No, they don't.
Tier 2 and 3 answers will vary.

D

1. Do you enjoy playing sports?
2. Do you like listening to music?
Tier 2 and 3 answers will vary.

Lesson C: Comparisons
pages 7–9

A

1. True. Martina likes watching TV more than playing cards.
2. False. Martina enjoys socializing less than cooking.
3. True. Ron likes reading less than watching TV.
4. True. Ron enjoys socializing as much as Martina does.
5. True. Frank likes cooking less than playing cards.
6. False. Frank enjoys watching TV less than socializing.

B

Answers will vary.

Lesson D: Reading pages 10–12

A

Jobs (nouns): architect, nurse, scientist, dancer, designer
Additional answers will vary.
Personality (adjectives): friendly, creative, quiet, shy, intellectual, outgoing
Additional answers will vary.
Activities (verbs): think, imagine, talk, meet, enjoy
Additional answers will vary.

B

(c) the right personality for the job

C

1. What does Gladys like doing? Meeting new people.
2. Who does Gladys enjoy talking to? Nurses and patients.
3. What does Phuong enjoy thinking about? Hard questions.
4. What does Phuong like doing? Reading.

5. What does Benito love writing? New songs.
6. Who does Benito like playing music with? His friends.

D

Answers will vary.

Lesson E: Writing pages 13–15

A

1. A counselor.
2. Outgoing and friendly.
3. Talking to people and helping them with their problems.
4. Answers will vary.

B

I think I have the right job for my personality. I'm a counselor. I work in a community center in Los Altos. I am a very outgoing person. I like talking to people. I am friendly. I enjoy helping people with their problems. I think a counselor is a good job for me because it fits my personality.

C

Eduardo has the right job for his personality. He is a counselor. He works in a community center in Los Altos. He is a very outgoing person. He likes talking to people. He is friendly. He enjoys helping people with their problems. He thinks a counselor is a good job for him because it fits his personality.

Lesson F: Another view
pages 16–18

A

1. Likes riding a motorcycle
   Likes camping
2. Loves playing guitar
   Enjoys gardening
3. Enjoys running
   Likes listening to music
4. Likes reading
   Loves painting

B

1. True. The shorter woman enjoys gardening.
2. False. The younger man enjoys running.
3. False. The older man likes camping.
4. True. The taller woman loves painting.
5. False. The shorter woman loves playing guitar.

C and D

Answers will vary.

Unit 2: At school

Lesson A: Get ready pages 19–21

A

1. Talk to your classmates. Ask questions in class.
2. Listen carefully and repeat. Listen to a pronunciation CD.
3. Write new words on index cards. Write new words in your notebook.
4. Study in a quiet room. Study in the library.
5. Make a list of tasks. Do important things first.
6. Go to bed early. Get up early.

B

Angela: Hi, Debbie. How's your English class?
Debbie: Not so good. I have too many things to do.
Angela: Don't feel discouraged. Make a list of tasks.
Debbie: A list is a good idea. It's hard to remember everything. I can't concentrate.
Angela: Maybe you need to study in a quiet place.
Debbie: Yeah, maybe the library. And I can't remember all these new words.
Angela: You should write new words on index cards.
Debbie: Yes, I should do that. This book is so boring, and I don't understand it.
Angela: Be more active when you read. Try to underline the main ideas.

Debbie: I'll try that. Thanks for your advice.
Tier 3 answers will vary.

Lesson B: Present perfect
pages 22–24

A

Regular verbs: lived, studied, talked, worked, wanted, moved
Irregular verbs: been, known, spoken, taught, had, done

B

1. Julie has worked since Feb. 1, 2007.
2. She has lived in San Antonio since Jan. 16, 2007.
3. She has lived in her apartment for one year and six months.
4. She has had her car for five months.
5. She has known her boyfriend since Dec. 1, 2007.
6. She has studied at the adult school for one day.

C

1. How long have you taught English?
2. How long have you lived in this town?
3. How long have you been in class today?
4. How long have you worked at this school?

Lesson C: Present perfect
pages 25–27

A

Regular verbs: asked, studied, tried, underlined, talked, concentrated
Additional answers will vary.
Irregular verbs: did, forgot, made, wrote, read, lost
Additional answers will vary.

B

1A. Have you ever asked for more homework?
1B. No, I haven't.
2A. Have they ever been late for school?
2B. No, they haven't.
3A. Has Marta ever spoken in class?
3B. Yes, she has.

4A. Has Peter ever done the wrong homework?
4B. Yes, he has.
5A. Has your teacher ever forgotten your name?
5B. No, she hasn't.
6A. Have you ever read a book in English?
6B. Yes, I have.
Tier 3 answers will vary.

C

1. Have you ever studied math?
2. Has she ever been to adult school?
3. Have they ever talked to the teacher?
4. Has he ever been late to school?
5. Have you ever forgotten your homework?
6. Has she ever taken the wrong bus?

Lesson D: Reading pages 28–30

A

Strategies: Guess the meaning of new words. Set a goal for reading every day. Talk about the story.
Examples: Use clues such as pictures and titles. Read two newspaper articles every day. OR Choose a book and read five pages every day. Tell a friend or your teacher about it.

B

1. (c) improving reading skills
2. (b) guess new words
3. (d) read every day
4. (a) understand it

C

Answers will vary.

Lesson E: Writing pages 31–33

A

Strategy: Plan your ideas. Check your work carefully.
Additional answer will vary.
Example: Use a chart or make a list. Underline mistakes in grammar.
Additional answer will vary.

I have read about some useful strategies for improving my writing. One strategy is to plan my ideas. For example, I can use a chart or make a list. Another strategy is to check my work carefully. For example, I can underline mistakes in grammar. I can't wait to try these new strategies, because I want to write English better.

Tier 2 and 3 answers will vary.

B

Tier 1: 5, 3, 4, 6, 1, 2

Tier 2 and 3 answers will vary.
Example answers:
Strategy: Talk to classmates.
Example: Ask them for advice about speaking English.

C

Answers will vary.
Example answer:

I have read about some useful strategies for speaking English. One strategy is to set a goal for using new words. For example, I can use five new words every day. Another strategy is to talk to classmates. For example, I can ask classmates for advice about speaking English. A third strategy is to be active in class. For example, I can volunteer to answer questions more often. I can't wait to try these new strategies, because I want to speak English better.

Lesson F: Another view
pages 34–36

A

Down	Across
1. answer	3. instructions
2. spend	5. easy
4. check	6. skim

B

Answers will vary.
Example answers:
1. (vocabulary) Buy a good dictionary.
2. (reading) Underline the main ideas.

3. (pronunciation) Listen carefully and repeat new words.
4. (listening) Watch TV in English.
5. (writing) Plan your ideas.

Unit 3: Friends and family

Lesson A: Get ready pages 37–39

A

1A. I need a favor.
1B. Sure. What do you need?
2A. I can't reach the light.
2B. You can borrow my ladder.
3A. My smoke alarm is beeping.
3B. You need to buy a new battery.
4A. I need quarters for the washing machine.
4B. I can lend you two quarters.

B

1. Maria lent a ladder to Ana.
2. Steve lent five dollars to Oscar.
3. My children borrowed some books from the teacher.
4. Manuela borrowed a dictionary from me.
5. Our neighbor lent some trash bags to us.
6. Lee-Hom lent a battery to you.

C

1. $48
2. $4
3. $200
4. Answers will vary.

Lesson B: *Because* and *because of* pages 40–42

A

1. Juan was late for work because of the traffic.
2. They couldn't play soccer because it was raining.
3. Simone couldn't sleep because it was noisy.
4. Rosanna studied a lot because she had an exam.
5. There was no school today because of the holiday.
6. The roads were closed because of an accident.

B

1. I couldn't find my door key because of the broken light.
2. We took our raincoats and umbrellas because the weather was bad.
3. We like the Mexican restaurant because the food is spicy.
4. Jim baked a cake for his wife because of her birthday.
5. Tina couldn't go to school today because she had a cold.

C and D

Answers will vary.

Lesson C: *Enough* and *too*
pages 43–45

A

1. I don't have time to bake a cake. I'm too busy.
2. I have trouble concentrating here. It's too noisy.
3. You need to wash those dishes again. They're not clean enough.
4. The exam started ten minutes ago. You're too late.
5. I don't like parties. I'm not outgoing enough.
6. My children watch TV every day. They're not active enough.
7. I can't buy a new TV. It's too expensive.
8. You should check your work again. You're not careful enough.

B

1. The weather is cold today. It's too cold to have a picnic.
2. My son is 12 years old. He's not old enough to drive.
3. The train left ten minutes ago. You're too late.
4. I sit at my desk all day. I'm not active enough.
5. The house has four bedrooms. It's large enough for the whole family.
6. I often make mistakes. I'm not careful enough.

C

Answers will vary.

Lesson D: Reading pages 46–48

A

Tier 1:
1. get away
2. went off
3. watch out (for)
4. broke into
5. get together
6. get into

Tiers 2 and 3:
1. went off
2. broke into
3. get away
4. get into
5. watch out
6. get together

B

1. (c) The neighbor called the police because she heard the alarm.
2. (a) The neighbor told the police she saw a tall man in a dark jacket.
3. (b) The writer and the neighbor are going to go out for dinner.
4. (c) The main idea of the article is: My neighbors watch out for each other.

C

Answers will vary.
Example answers:
I talk to my neighbors every day.
I stop my mail when I go away.

Lesson E: Writing pages 49–51

A

1. Can you please send a repair person?
2. Can you please clean it up?
3. Can you please fix it?
4. Can you please paint over it?
5. Can you please tell them to be quiet?
6. Can you please put in a new light?
Tier 3 answers will vary.

B

Tier 1:
3, 1, 4, 5, 2, 6
Tier 2:
3, 1, 7, 5, 9, 4, 2, 8, 6

Tier 3:
3, 1, 9, 5, 4, 2, 10, 8, 7, 11, 6

C

Tiers 1 and 2:
December 21, 2007

Greenway Properties
267 South Street
Richmond, VA 23228

To Whom It May Concern:
    I live at 233 Central Avenue, Apt. 12. My bathroom sink is leaking. Can you please send a repair person?
    Thank you in advance.

Sincerely,
Raymond D. Souza
Raymond D. Souza

Tier 3:
December 21, 2007

Greenway Properties
267 South Street
Richmond, VA 23228

To Whom It May Concern:
    I live at 233 Central Avenue, Apt. 12. My bathroom sink is leaking. Because of the leak, we are using too much water.
    Can you please send a repair person? I hope you will take care of this as soon as possible.
    Thank you in advance.

Sincerely,
Raymond D. Souza
Raymond D. Souza

Lesson F: Another view
pages 52–54

A

Ludmila: How many volunteers do you need?
Librarian: We need three volunteers.
Ludmila: How many hours a week can we work?
Librarian: You can work six hours a week.
Ludmila: What do volunteers do?
Librarian: They re-shelve books and help visitors to use the Internet.
Ludmila: What kind of experience do we need?
Librarian: You need to have computer experience.
Ludmila: When can I start?
Librarian: You can start immediately.

B

1. Neighborhood Fair: I can bake cookies.
2. Food Bank: I can collect food.
3. Animal Shelter: I can take care of animals.
4. Neighborhood Clean-up: I can pick up trash.
5. Children's Book Club: I can read stories to children.
6. Senior Care Center: I can talk to seniors.

C

Answers will vary.

Unit 4: Health

Lesson A: Get ready pages 55–57

A

Stan: Hello, doctor. I'm worried about my health.
Doctor: I see. What's the problem?
Stan: Well, I get enough sleep, but I feel tired all day.
Doctor: Maybe you're tired because you don't have a healthy diet. Have you gained weight?
Stan: Yes, I have. I think it's because I eat too much candy.
Doctor: That's possible. Do you get regular exercise?
Stan: Not really. I drive my car every day.
Doctor: Not enough exercise can also make you feel tired. Let's check your blood pressure now.

B

1. You should get more sleep.
2. You should get more exercise.
3. You should eat more fruit and vegetables.
4. You should talk to a doctor.
5. You should watch your diet.
Tier 3 answers will vary.

C

Answers will vary.

Lesson B: Present perfect
pages 58–60

A

1. Has Osman gone to the gym recently? Yes, he has.
2. Has Lucia lost weight lately? Yes, she has.
3. Has Alex eaten vegetables lately? No, he hasn't.
4. Have Osman and Alex visited the doctor recently? Yes, they have.
5. Have Lucia and Eva taken vitamins recently? No, they haven't.

B

Responses to questions will vary.
1. Have you checked your blood pressure recently? Yes, I have.
2. Have you visited a dentist lately?
3. Have you had a cold recently?
4. Have you taken vitamins recently?
5. Have you played soccer lately?
6. Have you eaten fish recently?
7. Answers will vary.
8. Answers will vary.

C

Answers will vary.

Lesson C: *Used to* pages 61–63

A

1. Steve used to play soccer, but now he plays baseball.
2. He used to eat potato chips, but now he eats fruit.
3. Marta used to drink soda, but now she drinks fruit juice.
4. She used to go to bed late, but now she goes to bed early.
5. Steve and Marta used to eat ice cream, but now they eat yogurt.
6. They used to ride bikes, but now they drive a car.

B

1. Did Steve use to play soccer? Yes, he did.
2. Did Steve use to eat fruit? No, he didn't.
3. Did Marta use to drink fruit juice? No, she didn't.

4. Did Marta use to go to bed late? Yes, she did.
5. Did Steve and Marta use to eat ice cream? Yes, they did.
6. Did Steve and Marta use to drive a car? No, they didn't.

C

Answers will vary.

Lesson D: Reading pages 64–66

A

1. prevent – verb
2. digestion – noun
3. herbal – adjective
4. treat – verb
5. sicknesses – noun

B

You can use garlic: when you cook soup, for high blood pressure, for insect bites, with fish or meat
You can use chamomile: to make tea, for colds and flu, to help digestion, to help you sleep

C

Answers will vary.

Lesson E: Writing pages 67–69

A

Mint is a popular herb in my country. The plant has small dark green leaves. It has a fresh smell. We used to grow mint in our garden when I was a child. We dried the leaves and made tea from them. It helps with indigestion and upset stomachs. We usually drank mint tea after every meal. Today, I make iced mint tea in the summer.

B

1. Mint is a popular herb.
2. It has small dark green leaves.
3. The writer grew mint in her garden.
4. The writer made tea from the leaves.
5. Mint tea is good for indigestion and upset stomachs.
6. The writer's family drank mint tea after every meal.
7. Today, the writer likes to make iced mint tea.

C

Lavender is a popular plant. It has silver-green leaves and tiny purple flowers. You can use the dried flowers to make tea. It helps with headaches. You can also make bath oil. It is very relaxing. Another use is to keep clothes fresh. The smell keeps moths away.

Tier 3 answer will vary.

Lesson F: Another view
pages 70–72

A

1. complaint: back pain, a headache, a sore throat
2. medication: aspirin, penicillin, ibuprofen
3. herbal supplement: garlic pills, echinacea, ginger
4. injury: a broken leg, a sprained ankle, a broken arm
5. illness: flu, a cold, asthma

B

Across	Down
1. gone	1. given
4. started	2. lost
5. gained	3. eaten

C

Answers will vary.

Unit 5: Around town

Lesson A: Get ready pages 73–75

A

1. exhibit: a presentation
2. concert: a performance of music or dance
3. tour: a short trip or guided walk
4. afford: to have enough money to buy something
5. admission: the price you pay to enter an event or place
6. options: choices

B

1. Leon loves paintings. He's going to the art exhibit.
2. Jun's children love stories. They're going to the storytelling at the library.
3. Sam loves flowers. He's going on the garden tour.

4. Khalid loves classical music. He's going to the piano concert.
5. Shamira loves dancing. She's going to the dance concert.
6. Rosita likes cooking. She's going to the community barbecue.

C

Answers will vary.
Example answer:
You: Let's go to the art exhibit at the museum.
Friend: Good idea! What time does it start?
You: It starts at 10:00 a.m.
Friend: How much is admission?
You: It costs $5.
Friend: OK. I'll meet you there.
You: If the weather is nice, we can go on a garden tour after the art exhibit.
Friend: Or we can go to a piano concert.
You: See you later, then.

Lesson B: Verbs + infinitives
pages 76–78

A

1A. What time did you agree to meet Cindy?
1B. I agreed to meet her at 5:00 p.m.
2A. How much can you afford to spend on the tickets?
2B. I can afford to spend about $20.
3A. Where do you like to go on weekends?
3B. We like to go to the park.
4A. When do you plan to take your vacation?
4B. I plan to take my vacation next week.
5A. What do you need to buy at the mall?
5B. I need to buy some new boots.
6A. What have you decided to wear to the party?
6B. I've decided to wear my red dress.

B

What does Wanda plan to do on Saturday? First, she plans to get up early because she wants to play tennis with Suzy. Then she needs to buy some food. She has agreed to have lunch with Charlie at 12:30 p.m. After lunch, they would like to visit the art museum. In the evening, she expects to meet Dina for dinner at 6:00 p.m. She has promised to go with Dina to a concert at 8:00 p.m. But the ticket is a little expensive, and she is worried that she can't afford to pay for it.

C

Answers will vary.

Lesson C: Present perfect
pages 79–81

A

1. The birthday party hasn't started yet.
2. Tom has set up the table already.
3. We have put up the decorations already.
4. I have made the food already.
5. You haven't brought out the food yet.
6. Our friends haven't arrived yet.

B

1A. It's 2:00 p.m. on Wednesday. Has the movie started yet?
1B. No, it hasn't.
2A. It's 3:30 p.m. on Wednesday. Has the movie ended yet?
2B. No, it hasn't.
3A. It's 9:00 p.m. on Friday. Has the concert begun already?
3B. Yes, it has.
4A. It's 5:00 p.m. on Saturday. Have the book vendors closed already?
4B. Yes, they have.
5A. It's 7:00 a.m. on Wednesday. Has the English café opened yet?
5B. No, it hasn't.
6A. It's November 6. Have the yoga classes started yet?
6B. Yes, they have.

Lesson D: Reading pages 82–84

A

1. The reviewer liked the second part of the fashion show.

2. Maria La Paz chose colors that were unremarkable.
3. The music for Maria La Paz's fashions was irritating.
4. Carlos Emanuel chose colors that were exciting.
5. The reviewer thought that Emanuel's show was sensational.

B

Positive words:
1. sensational: fantastic
4. amazing: great
5. superb: excellent

Negative words:
2. unremarkable: boring
3. irritating: unpleasant
6. excessive: too much

C

Answers will vary.

Lesson E: Writing pages 85–87

A

Baseball game
Positive information: The Tigers were incredible. The game was really exciting.
Negative information: The hot dogs were awful. The weather was cold and rainy. We didn't have umbrellas.

Rock concert
Positive information: The Classic Rockers were awesome. They are superb musicians. We had excellent seats near the stage.
Negative information: The sound level was too loud. I got a headache.

B

Hi Pete,
The baseball game on Saturday afternoon was fabulous. The Tigers were incredible. The game was really exciting. We ate hot dogs and popcorn. The hot dogs were awful. One problem: the weather. It was cold and rainy and we didn't have umbrellas. Come with us next time!
Andy

Hi Andy,

The rock concert on Saturday was fantastic. The Classic Rockers were awesome. They are superb musicians. We could see everything. We had excellent seats near the stage. One problem: the sound level. It was too loud and I got a headache. Come with us next time!
Pete

Lesson F: Another view
pages 88–90

A

1. Sasha loves to make herbal tea. She should take the Herbal Garden Tour. Admission is free.
2. David likes to take care of animals. He should go to the Animal Shelter Adoption Day. Admission is $5.
3. Rani needs to fix her kitchen sink. She should go to the Home Improvement Workshop. Admission is $20.
4. Beth used to study French. She should go to the French Film Festival. Admission is $15.

B

Across	Down
4. admission	1. awful
	2. amazing
	3. suberb
	4. exciting
	5. concert

Unit 6: Time

Lesson A: Get ready pages 91–93

A

1. deadline: date when something is due
2. impatient: anxious or restless
3. procrastinating: delaying
4. chores: tasks around the house
5. prioritize: put things in order of importance

B

Right now, I have many things to do. It is important to prioritize. I should make a to-do list. First, I have a lot of chores to do around the house. Secondly, my project is due tomorrow. The deadline is ten o'clock. When I hand in an assignment, I usually feel impatient because I want to know the result immediately. I also have to practice the piano because I have a concert next month. I need to manage my time better. Unfortunately, I'm good at procrastinating.

C

1. How many chores are on Veronica's list? There are five chores on Veronica's list.
2. What will she do first? She will clean the house first.
3. When is the deadline for her project? The deadline for her project is Monday.
4. What will she do if she has time? She will practice the guitar if she has time.

D

Answers will vary.

Lesson B: Dependent clauses
pages 94–96

A

1. When Ernesto has many things to do, he makes a to-do list.
2. When Felicia has to do some research, she goes on the Internet.
3. When I need to finish my work on time, I set a deadline.
4. When we have a test the next day, we go to bed early.
5. When they want to concentrate, they turn off the TV.

B

1. What does Ernesto do when he has many things to do? He makes a to-do list.
2. What does Felicia do when she has to do some research? She goes on the Internet.
3. What do you when you need to finish your work on time? I set a deadline.
4. What do you do when you have a test the next day? We go to bed early.
5. What do they do when they want to concentrate? They turn off the TV.

C

Answers will vary.

Lesson C: Dependent clauses
pages 97–99

A

1. After Sun-mi buys vegetables, she goes to work.
2. Sun-mi puts on her uniform before she starts work.
3. Before Sun-mi cooks the vegetables, she makes the dessert.
4. Sun-mi takes a break after she prepares the meal.

B

1. Sandy studies in the library before she goes to school.
2. After Sofia puts on her makeup, she goes to work.
3. Before Tam has breakfast, he reads the newspaper.
4. After Shin cooks dinner, she watches TV.

C

Answers will vary.

Lesson D: Reading pages 100–102

A

1. An organized person writes dates in a calendar.
2. An organized person isn't late for appointments.
3. A disorganized person is late for meetings.
4. A disorganized person doesn't feel irresponsible about losing things.
5. An organized person has enough time to do everything.
6. A disorganized person doesn't remember dates or times.

B

dis-: dishonest, disorganized
ir-: irresponsible, irregular
im-: impatient, impolite
un-: uncommon, unspoken
Additional answers will vary.

C

Answers will vary.

Lesson E: Writing pages 103–105

A

1. Disorganized people often forget their homework.
2. Impatient people get angry when you are late.
3. Impolite people don't say "thank you."
4. Organized people make a to-do list.
5. Patient people always wait for you.
6. Polite people always say "hello."

B

Samara is a very irresponsible person. She is always late for work. She never hands in her homework on time. When she borrows something, she doesn't give it back. When she is absent from class, she doesn't call the teacher to explain why. After she goes to a job interview, she doesn't write a thank-you note. In summary, Samara isn't very successful because she is irresponsible.

C

Gerald is a very responsible person. He is never late for work. He always hands in his homework on time. When he borrows something, he gives it back. When he is absent from class, he calls the teacher to explain why. After he goes to a job interview, he writes a thank-you note. In summary, Gerald is very successful because he is responsible.

Lesson F: Another view
pages 106–108

B

1. False. Ben spends the most time working.
2. False. He spends more time working than sleeping.
3. False. He spends the least time cooking and eating.
4. True. He spends less time sleeping than working.
5. False. He spends more time relaxing than cooking and eating.
6. Answers will vary.
7. Answers will vary.

C

Answers will vary.

Unit 7: Shopping

Lesson A: Get ready
pages 109–111

A

1. debt: money that you owe
2. interest: the cost of borrowing money
3. balance: the amount in your bank account
4. to pay off: to give back money that you owe
5. loan: money that you can borrow

B

1A. Why don't you like to borrow money?
1B. Because I don't want to get into debt.
2A. Why is it expensive to borrow money?
2B. Because you have to pay interest.
3A. How much is in your bank account?
3B. I'm not sure. I need to check my balance.
4A. I don't have enough money to buy a car.
4B. You could get a loan from the bank.
5A. I'm trying to save money.
5B. Are you planning to pay off your loan?

C

1. $100
2. $400

3. $250
4. Answers will vary.

D

Answers will vary.

Lesson B: Modals pages 112–114

A

1. Picture b.
   A. What could I do for my wife's birthday?
   B. You could bake a cake.
2. Picture d.
   A. I want to save more money.
   B. Why don't you cancel your credit cards?
3. Picture a.
   A. I want to buy a car.
   B. You could check the newspaper.
4. Picture c.
   A. I want to sell my sofa.
   B. You should advertise online.

B

1A. I spend too much money on cell phone calls.
1B. You could get a cheaper calling plan.
2A. I spend too much money on clothes.
2B. You could go to a thrift store. They have lots of different sizes and styles.
3A. I spend too much money on rent.
3B. You should find a cheaper apartment.
4A. I spend too much money on food.
4B. You should compare food prices before you shop.
Additional answers will vary.

C

Answers will vary.

Lesson C: Gerunds pages 115–117

A

1. I'm excited about starting school in the fall.
2. I'm afraid of losing my job.
3. I'm worried about paying my rent next month.

4. I'm happy about passing my exam last month.
5. I'm interested in learning about computers.
6. I'm tired of watching ads on TV.

B

1. What are you excited about?
2. What are you worried about?
3. What are you afraid of?
4. What are you interested in?

C

1. Denise is interested in buying a new car.
2. Francisco is afraid of losing his credit card.
3. What are you thinking about?
4. Are they worried about paying their bills?
5. What are you afraid of?
6. He's interested in buying a used car.

D

Answers will vary.

Lesson D: Reading pages 118–120

A

1. (b) how to save money
2. (c) make a list of your expenses
3. (b) controlling your spending
4. (a) people only pay the minimum

B

1. family - adjective; budget - noun
2. credit - adjective; card - noun
3. interest - adjective; rate - noun
4. minimum - adjective; payment - noun
5. thrift - adjective; store - noun

C

Answers will vary.

Lesson E: Writing pages 121–123

A

1. Dear Money Man,
   We bought a new car two months ago, but now it is very difficult for us to make the payments. Gas prices have gone up and we cannot afford the gas. We are driving my old car because it uses less gas. What should we do?
   Two-car Dad

2. Dear Money Man,
   My daughter spends too much time on her cell phone. She talks to her friends all day and all night. I bought it for her because I can contact her any time, but the phone bills are too high! What should I do?
   Worried Mom

3. Dear Money Man,
   I go to the mall every weekend and I always buy new clothes for myself. I don't really need them and I can't afford them. I have bags of new clothes in my closet. I never wear them, but I'm too shy to take them back to the store. What should I do?
   Clothes Crazy

B

Letter 1: You should exchange your car. You should sell your new car.
Letter 2: You should give her a phone budget. Your daughter should pay her own phone bills.
Letter 3: You should stop going to the mall. You should cancel your credit cards.
Tier 3 answers will vary.

C

Sample answer:
Dear Clothes Crazy,
   It's important to have clothes, but you don't need to spend all your money on them. I have a few suggestions. First, you could stop going to the mall on weekends. Next, you could shop at a thrift store when you need new clothes. Finally, you could give your extra clothes away.
   The Money Man

Lesson F: Another view pages 124–126

A

1. Ace
2. Star
3. Ace
4. Star
5. Star
6. Ace
7. Star
8. Ace

B

This person spends a lot of money:
I like to eat out. I use more than two credit cards. I spend a lot of time on the phone. I make the minimum credit card payment. I like to buy new clothes every week.
This person saves a lot of money:
I pay cash for everything. I save money in the bank every month. I compare prices online. I use coupons to get a discount. I only buy things on sale.

Additional answers will vary.

Unit 8: Work

Lesson A: Get ready
pages 127–129

A

Manager: Good morning. Please come in and sit down.
Claudia: Thank you.
Manager: My name is Andrew Gladstone. I'm the personnel manager.
Claudia: Pleased to meet you.
Manager: Which job are you applying for?
Claudia: I'm applying for the job of sales manager.
Manager: I see. And what is your current job?
Claudia: I'm working in an Internet sales company.
Manager: How long have you been working there?
Claudia: For about a year.
Manager: Which shift do you prefer?
Claudia: I prefer the day shift.

B

Manager: Tell me about your background.
Claudia: I am from Brazil.
Manager: What are your strengths?

Claudia: I am reliable. I get along well with others.
Manager: What skills do you have?
Claudia: I studied computers. I speak Portuguese.
Additional answers will vary.

Lesson B: Present perfect continuous pages 130–132

A

For: two days, three years, a long time, an hour, five hours, ten weeks, a month
Since: 3:00 p.m., September, July 12th, 2002, yesterday, Friday, this morning
Additional answers will vary.

B

1. I have been working here for six weeks.
2. We have been using computers for five years.
3. Rick has been looking for a job since July.
4. Serena has been studying art since 2004.
5. Tina and Tam have been fixing the car for three hours.
6. You have been talking on the phone for 40 minutes.

C

1. How long have you been working here?
2. Have you been waiting for a long time?
3. We have been painting this house since Monday.
4. Has Tran been studying for a long time?
5. How long have we been waiting here?
6. Denis and Jean have been talking all morning.

Lesson C: Phrasal verbs pages 133–135

A

1. Victor is going to throw them out.
2. The teacher is handing it out.
3. I am going to call her back.
4. Alex is turning them off.
5. We are going to clean it up.
6. Can you please turn it up?

B

1. *call back:* a friend, a relative, my husband, the doctor
2. *throw away:* old newspapers, trash, a broken cup, old shoes
3. *clean up:* the kitchen, the classroom, the house, the lunchroom
4. *turn down:* the TV, the music, the volume, the heat
5. *fill out:* a job application, a form, a work order, a survey

C

1. You don't need the dictionary. Please put it away.
2. The kitchen is dirty. Please clean it up.
3. The TV is too loud. Please turn it down.
4. Your brother called this morning. Please call him back.
5. You don't need these old shoes. Please throw them away.
6. Here is the application. Please fill it out.

Lesson D: Reading pages 136–138

A

1. critical: very important
2. to network: to get to know other people
3. a fair: a gathering or conference
4. patient: calm or uncomplaining
5. firm: very strong
6. confidence: a belief in yourself

B

1. critical
2. firm
3. network
4. confidence
5. fair
6. patient

C

1. Ana has been keeping a blog because she wants to remember this time.
2. Ana tried to show confidence because she was with her co-workers.
3. Ana was confused because her job wasn't what they told her.
4. Ana has been asking questions because she's not sure about the job.

Lesson E: Writing pages 139–141

A

(1) Your address
(2) The date
(3) The name of the person you are writing to
(4) The address of the person you are writing to
(5) Dear . . .
(6) The reason you are writing
(7) Sincerely,
(8) Signature
(9) Your name

B

Tier 1: 4, 6, 2, 3, 5, 1
Tier 2:

> 48 South Street
> Albany, NY 12224
> June 26, 2008

Andrew Gladstone,
    Personnel Manager
SmartZone Department Store
1564 Central Ave.
Albany, NY 12210

Dear Mr. Gladstone:
    I would like to thank you for the job interview I had with you on June 25. I appreciate the time you spent with me. Thank you for giving me information about the job of sales manager. It sounds very interesting.
    Thank you again for your time. I hope to hear from you soon.

Sincerely,
Claudia Silva
Claudia Silva

Tier 3 answer will vary.

Lesson F: Another view pages 142–**144**

A

1. True. Martin has better eye contact than Rosita.
2. False. Rosita speaks more slowly and clearly than Martin.

3. False. Martin is more enthusiastic than Rosita.
4. True. Martin needs to improve his speaking.
5. True. Rosita needs to improve her eye contact.
6. False. The interviewer thinks Martin should get the job.

B
1. What job are you applying for? I'm applying for the job of customer service manager.
2. What is your current job? I'm working as a hotel desk clerk.
3. What skills do you have? I can use a computer and I speak three languages.
4. Why should I hire you? Because I'm friendly and outgoing, and I love working with people.

Unit 9: Daily living

Lesson A: Get ready
pages 145–147

A

Dear Neighbors,

Are you worried about crime in our neighborhood? Join our Neighborhood Watch and help make our neighborhood safer. Here are stories from some of our neighbors.

"Some people broke into our garage while we were on vacation last summer and stole our car."

"Someone robbed my grocery store and took all the cash from the safe."

"Robbers got in through the bathroom window. They stole our computer, TV, and DVD player."

"Someone wrote graffiti on the front of my home and threw trash into the garden. Now I have to clean up the mess."

We all know that our neighborhood is getting more dangerous. Help us to reduce crime. Join the Neighborhood Watch! Call 555-6726 to find out more.

B
1. What did robbers steal from the garage? They stole a car.

2. What did someone take from the grocery store? Someone took all the cash.
3. How did robbers get into one home? They got in through the bathroom window.
4. What are the neighbors worried about? They're worried about crime in their neighborhood.
5. What should the neighbors do? They should join the Neighborhood Watch.

C

Answers will vary.

Lesson B: Past continuous
pages 148–150

A
1. Was Tina cooking dinner? Yes, she was.
2. What was Dino doing? He was talking on the phone.
3. Was Frank talking on the phone? No, he wasn't.
4. What was Pauline doing? She was e-mailing her friends.
5. Were Sam and Luisa cooking dinner? No, they weren't.
6. What were Sam and Luisa doing? They were babysitting.

B
1. What was Beth doing yesterday morning?
2. Teresa and Jimmy were watching TV all day.
3. I was talking with my friend on Monday night.
4. Was he writing a letter?
5. What were you wearing yesterday?
6. I was baking a cake for my daughter.

C

Answers will vary.

Lesson C: Past continuous and simple past pages 151–153

A
1. Julia was working in the garden when she saw the fire.
2. I was driving too fast around a corner when I hit a tree.

3. While Frank was cooking dinner, his sister called.
4. The fire alarm went off while we were taking a break.
5. When the burglar broke into the house, they were visiting the neighbors.
6. When the rain started, we were studying in the library.

B
1. Bill heard a noise in the garden while he was eating dinner.
2. Bohai and Sofia phoned their friends while they were waiting for a bus.
3. Liana and I were taking a test when we heard the fire alarm.
4. When Teresa broke her tooth, she was eating a sandwich.
5. Mr. and Mrs. Ramirez were carrying a lot of bags when they came home.
6. While Joe and Omar were jogging in the park, they saw a deer.

C

Answers will vary.

Lesson D: Reading
pages 154–156

A
1. gathering: collecting
2. to evacuate: leave a dangerous place
3. generous: helpful and giving
4. strangers: people you don't know
5. destroyed: completely damaged
6. grabbed: took quickly

B
1. gathering
2. grabbed
3. evacuate
4. strangers
5. generous
6. destroyed

C
(1) We heard a fire alarm.
(2) The fire engines arrived.
(3) We grabbed our documents and some clothes.

(4) We evacuated our apartment.
(5) We ran downstairs.
(6) Some strangers talked to us.
(7) We stayed with my parents.
(8) We moved into a new apartment.

D

Answers will vary.

Lesson E: Writing
pages 157–159

A

1. What is the story about? The story is about a woman, a rabbit, and a dog.
2. When did the story happen? Two days ago.
3. Where did it happen? Near the lake.
4. What was the woman doing? She was walking her dog.
5. What happened? The dog chased a rabbit into the lake.
6. Why was the woman worried? Because her dog was swimming in the lake.
7. How did they story end? The dog saved the rabbit.

B

Answers will vary.

Lesson F: Another view
pages 160–162

A

1. True. Good street lighting is most important for the Gomez family.
2. False. Helpful neighbors are most important for the Park family.
3. True. Helpful neighbors are more important for the Park family than for the Gomez family.
4. False. Good street lighting is more important for the Gomez family than for the Park family.
5. False. Home security alarms have the same importance for both families.

B

1. You need an emergency exit map to find the exit.

2. You need a fire extinguisher to put out a fire.
3. You need a fire alarm to warn everyone to evacuate.
4. You need a first-aid kit to help someone with an injury.
5. You need emergency exit signs to see the exits clearly.

Tier 3 answers will vary.

C

Answers will vary.

Unit 10: Leisure

Lesson A: Get ready
pages 163–165

A

Jenny: I want to ask my boss for a few days off next week. I really need a vacation.
Ramona: That's a good idea! Where do you want to go?
Jenny: I want to go to New York, but I don't have enough money to fly.
Ramona: If you book a flight in advance, you can get a discount.
Jenny: I know, but the hotels are very expensive, too.
Ramona: That's true. With room tax, it can be over $200 a night. Why don't you stay somewhere cheaper?
Jenny: That's a good idea. I could go camping instead. I'd like to go to the beach. A round-trip ticket by bus is only $60.
Ramona: You'll need to reserve a campsite before you go. But it will be much cheaper than New York.
Jenny: And more relaxing, too!

B

1. Hannah and Mark: $79
2. Katerina: $78

C

Answers will vary.

Lesson B: Dependent clauses
pages 166–168

A

1. If I find a cheap air ticket, I'll fly to Costa Rica.

2. What will you do if you get a few days off?
3. We won't go to the concert if the tickets are too expensive.
4. They will go skiing if there is enough snow.
5. If they don't find a hotel, they'll go camping.
6. If Rita has enough time, she'll visit a museum.

B

1. What will Pete do if he saves some money?
2. What will Janine buy if she goes to the mall?
3. Where will Ron go if he gets a vacation?
4. What will Carlos do if he doesn't go to the movies?
5. Where will Anna and her family go if it doesn't rain on Saturday?
6. What will Len and Flora wear if they go to the party?

C

1. If we have a few days off, we will go camping.
2. If it snows, we'll take our snow boots.
3. They will take a vacation if prices are not too high.
4. I won't go swimming if it rains.
5. Julio won't go to the party if it starts too late.
6. Barbara will take the children to the zoo if she has time.

Lesson C: Dependent clauses
pages 169–171

A

1. Before I travel to Italy, I'll study Italian.
2. Before Vera goes camping, she'll buy a tent.
3. After Angela arrives at the airport, she'll call her parents.
4. Pablo and Jun will make a fire after they collect some wood.
5. Wanda will get a new cell phone before she flies to Europe.
6. After we eat breakfast, we'll pay our hotel bill.

Tier 3 answers will vary.

B

1. After I learn French, I'll go to Paris.
2. Luis and Pablo will check into their hotel before they buy a street map.
3. After Aleesha visits her cousins in Florida, she will go on vacation.
4. We will have lunch after we take the city tour.
5. Before Sam and Cindy go to a dance club, they will eat dinner.
6. Omar will watch a movie after he finishes packing his suitcase.

C

Answers will vary.

Lesson D: Reading
pages 172–174

A

1. attraction: a place that tourists like to visit
2. admission: the cost of the ticket
3. in advance: before
4. to sell out: to finish the supply of tickets
5. to escape: to get away
6. ferries: special boats to carry people and cars

B

1. escape
2. ferries
3. in advance
4. sell out
5. attraction
6. admission

C

1. (b) An island.
2. (a) It's cool.
3. (c) Ferry tickets.
4. (b) Cycling, swimming, walking and bird watching.

Lesson E: Writing pages 175–177

A

One of the most popular zoos in the Midwest is Lincoln Park Zoo in Chicago, Illinois. It is located on North Clark Street near the center of the city. It is open from 10:00 a.m. to 7:00 p.m. every day except Mondays. Admission is free. The zoo has something for everyone. It has animals from all over the world. If you like elephants and tigers, you can go on the African safari ride. If you like birds, you will enjoy the scenic paddleboat cruise. If you have children, they will love the Story Time entertainment. If you want to relax, you can go to the Big Cats Café and enjoy ice cream. At the end of your visit, you can buy gifts in the zoo store. Children and adults love to visit Lincoln Park Zoo.

B

1. Things you can do at Lincoln Park Zoo
2. You can see elephants and tigers. You can go on an African safari. You can go on a cruise. You can eat ice cream. You can listen to children's stories.
3. You can buy gifts in the zoo store.

C

Answers will vary.

Lesson F: Another view
pages 178–180

A

Across	Down
1. reserve	2. vacation
3. hotel	4. tourist
5. attraction	
6. admission	

B

Answers will vary.

Illustration credits